Intuitive Parenting

"Debra Snyder embodies HeartGlow! Her authentic, intuitive, expansive, and compassionate self infuses her book. The insights and honesty of Debra's journey resonate throughout this book—there is wisdom here for all of us."

JOYCE WHITELEY HAWKES, PhD, author of *Cell-Level Healing*

"Touching, tender, truthful. . . . HeartGlow is an intuitive parenting program, which can maintain the spiritual connection for the whole family. The story of triumph is wonderful. The lessons for deepening the parent/child connection through intuition is a bonus."

DR. CARON GOODE, author of *Raising Intuitive Children* and *Nurture Your Child's Gift*

"*Intuitive Parenting* is authentically powerful. Wonderfully written and masterfully compiled, *Intuitive Parenting* offers valuable insights in embracing an intuitive approach with children and your family."

JENNIFER CREWS, MA, child intuitive, contributing author of *Power of the Magdalene*, columnist for *Children of the New Earth Magazine*, live radio talk show host

"*Intuitive Parenting* is transformative. It can help any loving parent become more insightful and intuitive, while touching all readers with its warmth and inspiration."

DR. PAUL COLEMAN, author of *The 30 Secrets of Happily Married Couples* and *We Need to Talk*

Intuitive Parenting

LISTENING TO THE WISDOM OF YOUR HEART

Intuitive Parenting

Debra J. Snyder, PhD

Foreword by Paul Coleman, PsyD

ATRIA PAPERBACK
New York London Toronto Sydney

BEYOND WORDS
Hillsboro, Oregon

ATRIA PAPERBACK
A Division of Simon & Schuster, Inc.
1230 Avenue of the Americas
New York, NY 10020

BEYOND WORDS
20827 N.W. Cornell Road, Suite 500
Hillsboro, Oregon 97124-9808
503-531-8700 / 503-531-8773 fax
www.beyondword.com

Managing editor: Lindsay S. Brown
Copyeditor: Ali McCart
Design: Devon Smith
Proofreader: Marvin Moore
Composition: William H. Brunson Typography Services

First Atria Paperback/Beyond Words trade paperback edition May 2010

Manufactured in the United States of America

10 9 8 7 6 5 4 3 2 1

Library of Congress Cataloging-in-Publication Data

Snyder, Debra J.
    Intuitive parenting : listening to the wisdom of your heart / Debra J. Snyder.
        p.   cm.
    Includes bibliographical references.
    1. Parenting.   2. Parent and child.   3. Intuition.   I. Title.
    HQ755.8.S6433   2010
    649'.151—dc22

                                                                    2009050208

ISBN: 978-1-58270-250-6
ISBN: 978-1-4391-6355-9 (ebook)

The corporate mission of Beyond Words Publishing, Inc.: *Inspire to Integrity*

I dedicate this book to the children, the carriers of the light.
Although the journeys can be difficult, your pure radiance
illuminates our paths, leading us to a remarkable place
of joy, grace, and love.

Thank you for showing us the way home.

TO SEE AS GOD SEES

It is your destiny to see as God sees,
to know as God knows,
to feel as God feels.

How is this possible? How?
Because divine love cannot defy its very self.

Divine love will be eternally true to its own being,
and its being is giving all it can,
at the perfect moment.

And the greatest gift
God can give is His own experience.

Every object, every creature, every man, woman and child
has a soul and it is the destiny of all,
to see as God sees, to know as God knows,
to feel as God feels, to Be
As God Is.

—MEISTER ECKHART, ANCIENT MYSTIC (1260–1328)

Contents

Foreword

The sound of creek water moving over rocks—it remains one of my favorite sounds in nature, where the hard things of life are no longer obstacles but musical instruments played upon by rushing waters, creating a noise so wonderful and peaceful, I could sit and listen for hours.

I sat next to Deb Snyder one day at a workshop for psychic development. She introduced herself, and we immediately began speaking as if we had met before. We hadn't, but I've had encounters with people who were loving, gracious, compassionate, funny, wise, sincere—Deb was all of those—so she was no stranger, after all. And as we spoke occasionally throughout the weekend, I listened to her touching and powerful stories about her daughter, Raegan; her husband, Mark, and the remarkable and inspiring journey they were on. While I may have been listening to her words, what I heard was the tranquil sound of water over rocks. She and her family were encountering life's hard times yet had managed to keep moving forward—over, under, around—undaunted by obstacles, filled with love and the faith that their journey had meaning and Divine purpose.

"The world breaks everyone," Hemingway concluded. "And afterward many are strong at the broken places." His is a hopeful and poetic sentiment. But if I were to call up Deb this minute and try to apply that outlook to her life, she would be puzzled. "But nothing has been broken," I can imagine her saying.

Her daughter, Raegan, was born in 1999 with a rare brain malformation that to some would be a story of hardship and heartbreak. But with Deb, Mark, and Raegan, there are no broken places and no broken hearts. To be sure, they suffered through fear and the pain parents feel for a child who has not been spared life's most difficult challenges. Raegan cannot see, can verbalize just a few words, experiences seizures daily, and requires a gastric tube to receive nourishment—yet through a telepathic process at age two, she was able to reveal to Debra that she, Raegan, had developed a life-threatening medical problem overlooked by her doctors. Debra intuitively trusted that Raegan was indeed—and inexplicably—communicating to her and alerted the physicians in time to save Raegan's life.

You want mystical? You want to believe in angels and the beautiful world of our soul? You want love, hearth, and home? You've come to the right book.

Intuitive Parenting is Dr. Debra Snyder's gift to parents everywhere, and particularly to parents of special-needs children. You've heard of mother's intuition (and on behalf of fathers everywhere, we dads are intuitive too), but *Intuitive Parenting* isn't about how to be more observant with your usual senses or how to pick up on your child's nonverbal cues. Instead it makes a quantum leap forward and reveals that you—a loving parent or caregiver—can open up energy centers inside yourself and be able to communicate telepathically with your children and understand them using abilities beyond your usual five senses. (And your children have already communicated that way to you!) You may not believe you are clairvoyant or telepathic. But with Debra's guidance and with the secret ingredient you hold—your love for your children—you will be amazed at what your soul can do.

You have all heard stories of moms or dads who awaken out of a sound sleep and just *know* something is wrong. And when they investigate, they discover they were able to help their child in the nick of time. Even if you have never experienced it yourself, you probably nod your head knowing full well that parents and their children are highly tuned in to one another, almost mystically so— and that capability can easily be strengthened. That's one of the interesting points of Deb's book—it discusses that sense of what I call "knowing without knowing how you know," and you find yourself both marveling at what seems so unusual and rare—and yet you instinctively *know* it is a real, active part of our very makeup. Telepathy, clairvoyance, knowing without knowing how you know—it's in you. In fact, it *is* you. It's your soul.

I am a psychologist in private practice and have authored numerous books on how to make your relationships work. I was trained in the scientific method—which means to be skeptical and let the data speak for itself—but was raised by wonderful, wise, and loving parents who never let me forget there was more to each of us beyond our earthly body. Like Debra Snyder, there were times earlier in my life when I just knew things I shouldn't have known. At times it was fun, but usually it made me uneasy. After my dad passed away in 1995, he found ways to communicate to me—beyond what could be called wishful thinking on my part—which erased my unease and further opened my eyes to the mystical. I estimate I have conducted over forty thousand psychotherapy sessions thus far, and there were times I chalked up my clinical intuition to mere clinical experience. I was so practiced at listening to people and helping them that my intuition about them was really not intuition but experience—or so I convinced myself. It was only when I began telling some of my clients things about themselves that I shouldn't have known—such as how one's deceased mother had once fallen on the ice and suffered a head injury, or how one's deceased dad used to have a passion for Clydesdale horses and was lovingly teased about his oversized earlobes—that I realized so much more than clinical expertise was occurring in my office. So now I quietly go about my business as a psychologist *and* a part-time psychic medium. Hamlet was right. There are more things in heaven and earth than are dreamt of in our philosophies.

I encourage you to listen closely to all Dr. Debra Snyder has to offer in her remarkable and groundbreaking book. I say this not just on account of my life experiences—my roles as husband, dad, psychologist, and author, and my experiences with the mystical—but also because of my unshakable faith that the Divine exists, that the Divine is Love, and that we are all meant to uncover our soul's purpose and live a life of meaning despite the obstacles we inevitably face. Even if your life has met with tragedies—*especially* if there have been tragedies—when you read *Intuitive Parenting* you will begin to believe what Debra says— that we are all "priceless works of art" and that we are not defined and limited by our stories of woe or hardship. We can transcend them. When you develop a spiritual understanding of your child's journey from deep within your heart, you discover that what is truly meaningful in your life is often not found in the grand palaces we often seek or with Nobel Prize–worthy accomplishments. Rather, what is truly meaningful often exists in small rooms, sleeps in out-of-the-way places, and is tended by people with warm hearts on cold nights.

Foreword

There is warmth, tenderness, love, and God's presence in the home of Debra Snyder; her husband, Mark; and their daughter, Raegan. Finding those very qualities and living them—that's what we're all here for. We are all water moving over rocks. . . .

Paul Coleman, PsyD
www.paul-coleman.com

Preface

It has been my honor and sincere privilege to share the personal story of life with my daughter, Raegan Aria. The details presented here are truthful and accurate to my direct experience and perception. I have, however, changed names, descriptions, and certain locations in some circumstances to protect the privacy and identity of the actual people involved. It is my greatest wish for these accounts to open hearts, promoting unity, acceptance, and understanding. We are grateful for the diverse experiences and opportunities our lives have given us and choose to live each day in celebration of the Divine light within. Thank you for coming along with us on this HeartGlow journey.

Acknowledgments

I would like to express my sincere gratitude to the numerous loving people who have assisted me along the way and have made this book a reality. To my amazing daughter, Raegan Aria, who has introduced me to new worlds and truly taught me how to love. To my husband, Mark Storck, for all the years, all the tears, all the smiles, and for his constant devotion to our girl. To my mom, Connie Polomski, for her unyielding love, dedication, and strength in everything she does. To my son, Graham, and his wife, Brooke, for their smiles and jubilant energy. To my dad, Jim Snyder, and his wife, Linda, for their love and humor. To Mark's mom, Barbara Storck, for her grace and kind heart. To my "gamma" Jean McInnis for always being there for me. My love and appreciation goes out to the many members of our extended family and our family of friends, nurses, doctors, therapists, and teachers who celebrate daily life with us. I honor you all from the depths of my being.

Acknowledgments

I especially want to thank the many people who supported my decision to write this book and embark on such an unusual vocation. To Lindsay Neithercut for over twenty-five years of your loving friendship and wild antics. To Gloria Cadman for being the perfect person to share with us the care and nurturing of my daughter. To Carl Walsh for always being able to capture the beauty. To my agent, Sammie Justesen, for seeing the book's potential and finding its proper home. To Cynthia Black, Richard Cohn, Marie Hix, and my publishing family at Beyond Words for appreciating the heart in this work and helping me to share it with the world. To the AngelBabyMoms for being everything you are to your children and to me. To the HeartGlow team and members of the Maine Center for Spiritual Enrichment, you will always be my foundation and ever so dear to my heart. To Dr. Paul Coleman for your encouragement and patience in answering so many of my pesky questions. To David Nicholson for your technical expertise, the double cheeseburgers, and always your Qi. To my friends, mentors, clients, and energy colleagues for your support, wisdom, and poignant reflections over the years. I love you all.

The very best reason parents are so special . . . because we are the holders of a priceless gift, a gift we received from countless generations we never knew, a gift that only we now possess and only we can give to our children. That unique gift, of course, is the gift of ourselves. Whatever we can do to give that gift, and to help others receive it, is worth the challenge of all our human endeavor.

FRED ROGERS, *MISTER ROGERS TALKS WITH PARENTS*

PART I

Setting the Tone: It's All Energy

1

Exceptional Teachers: Our Children as Our Guides

Only those who look with the eyes of children
can lose themselves in the object of their wonder.

EBERHARD ARNOLD

The world has no better display of grace than a parent caring for a child, and the child himself—vulnerable and trusting, exhibiting faith, peace, and reliance on the Universe. If you're picking this book up, it means that you're looking to deepen the communication between yourself and the children you love. In my experience working with a wide variety of new parents, parents of special-needs children, or more spiritually minded parents who wish to enrich their relationships, I have found that one element remains the same throughout: our children, each and every one, are our teachers and guides.

My wish is for parents to see the relationship with their children in a new light, with increased awareness and depth. Learning to acknowledge children as soul beings with vast innate knowledge gives us a key to greater joy in life; they are innocents, the freshest perspectives with which we will have the privilege of interacting. You will soon discover profound spiritual mysteries can be found in the stillness of the morning, rocking a crying child, and in the simplest of everyday situations. Whether you are a first time parent or seasoned expert, this book will help you understand that our children have much to teach us. I believe that all children live in the resonance of God's love, and they show us how to transcend our perceptions, look beyond the fragmented self, and attune to the concept of Universal Oneness. Their trust and inborn love show us that we are all connected—each of us beautiful, essential parts of the Divine whole.

These concepts may seem too ethereal or "out there" for you. Yet you may find that parenting is a journey to an unknown but wonderful destination—a place where you will surprisingly arrive with much joy, finding that your beliefs about the world have shifted. Mine certainly did after the birth of my daughter, and in ways I never could have imagined. Heart communication, energy healing, and intuitive parenting are intrinsic abilities that have become undeveloped and devalued in our fast-paced, have-it-all-now culture. Yet our children come to energy awareness naturally, right from the start.

This form of connection and communication is not a talent or gift reserved for shamans, mediums, or psychics, although these highly sensitive individuals can be encouraging role models because they demonstrate the possibilities awaiting you when you begin to develop your own sensitivities. Parents of any background and any situation can utilize heightened energy skills to connect with their children at levels never before explored, getting to know them on a soul level. The energy inherent in the parent-child relationship plays a crucial role in communication. You can develop a greater energy connection with your child and dramatically improve your family's quality of life through intuitive parenting, and you can begin to experience this connection today.

Many people have had glimpses into the power of intuition through meaningful coincidences or simple hunches that have paid off. The cliché *mother's intuition* is known in nearly every culture, and it explains a bond no one dares deny. Now is the time to step it up a notch by cultivating your inherent skill and putting it into action. Fathers can also benefit from these teachings in unique ways, learning how to bond with their child and open the flow of communication.

We've all been given the potential to parent with intuitive hearts; our children are patiently waiting for us to experience the higher clarity only a glowing, divine heart can give. To illustrate the techniques used in this book, I want to share my own story, which shows how intuitive parenting can unfold in even the most trying circumstances. It is my own darling daughter who has challenged me to walk such an unconventional path and journey to destinations far beyond my imagination. Our compelling intuitive connection prompted me to obtain my doctorate in metaphysical philosophy and immerse myself in the science and theories behind energy communication, spirituality, and consciousness. Along with the tips, exercises, and various tools that I developed to enhance this intuitive connection, you will also find the spirited journey of a child who has taught her parents to live, love, and celebrate every moment—a vibrant child unable to walk, talk, or develop normally, yet able to transcend conventional wisdom to save her own life by speaking through her heart.

This child, my daughter, Raegan Aria, shows the world how children intuitively draw upon the Divine energy source and bring forth awareness to those willing to listen with a loving heart. She teaches how this same source emanates through all of us as well and can be firmly established into our consciousness by our thoughts, decisions, and actions. It is my hope that the experiences we share in this book will inspire you in your journey to discovering the potential in intuitive parenting.

Divine guidance comes to us openly and freely in myriad ways, but we must use energy expertise to decipher the messages delivered through our hearts. My journey with Raegan led me to write this book and develop an intuitive energy protocol for parents to use in their own homes. This method takes mother's intuition to the next level by empowering and educating parents on playing an active role in healing through enhancing communication with their children via their subtle energy system. As a parent, teacher, friend, or caregiver, you can use your intuitive heart, your *HeartGlow*, to perceive, interpret, and act on information not accessible by other means: You will just *know*.

This method has been developed through in-depth study, experience, and daily practical application with my own and other families, coupled with my studies in metaphysics, interpersonal relationships, energy communication, and holistic living. These methods unlock a new door to healing and communication for families by bridging the emerging scientific knowledge of energy medicine with holistic, traditional, and spiritual approaches. Life truly takes on a new dimension when we feel the glow of an intuitive heart.

BAPTISM BY FIRE

At one time, energy didn't seem to play a role in my life. To me, the word *energy* referred to the utility company, or maybe a source of fuel. I never gave a second thought to human energy or biofields. I was, however, familiar with being intuitive or psychic. As a young child, I knew things. I felt things. Often I would know insignificant details about casual matters, and at other times I was able to see through facades to the intentions in people's hearts. I could pick out a liar at a thousand yards. I didn't realize this was an unusual trait, because many of my family members could do similar feats. We didn't study or hold theories about our gifts, we just used them. It was like breathing air; you do it all the time but don't exactly know how.

For twenty-nine years I went through life as a casual intuitive. My insights slowly dwindled as my intellectual and logical side grew stronger. I didn't notice the departure, since I was wrapped up in school, work, and relationships. Things outside myself held greater importance, so my inner glow dimmed from lack of nourishment and use. Like most people, I contented myself with the daily pursuit of happiness through hard work and obtaining possessions. Shouldn't that make me happy? It never occurred to me that there were dimensions of happiness I'd never heard of. I certainly didn't expect my newborn child would be my spiritual guide to uncharted corners of the Universe.

Like most couples, my husband, Mark, and I had experienced good times and bad. We thought we'd gone through just about everything in our eleven years together. Now, confronted with the unbearable illness of our newborn daughter, we didn't know what to say to each other. We felt numb from the constant barrage of negativity.

The birth of my daughter triggered an immediate, dramatic shift in our perspective on life. I felt as though a massive earthquake had turned my entire world upside down. Each new medical specialist brought a frightening tremor. Every diagnostic test was a startling shake. Mark and I had no idea who we were, what we should be doing, or how we fit into this altered world. Our thoughts and dreams about the birth of our child came crashing down around us, replaced by a frightening, unpredictable reality. To think I'd been concerned about rattles and baby buntings!

Mark, an upbeat and earthy person by nature, has a habit of whistling—a behavior I took for granted after all the years we'd known each other. He would whistle in the shower, while cooking dinner, working in the yard, or just lying on the couch. To be honest, I found it sweet, yet annoying after a few moments, and I teased him relentlessly about it. When his pitch got especially high, it hurt my ears and drove me absolutely nuts. Now, as we sat in the stale hospital room, Mark didn't whistle. He didn't sing or hum. For the first time in our lives together, he was silent, and it frightened me. The song in his heart was as quiet and fragile as our new baby girl. I prayed to feel his exuberant energy and hear him whistle his heart song again.

If I were to pinpoint the exact moment during our hospital experience I feared my baby wouldn't come home and see the room we so tenderly prepared for her, it was when I saw the expression on the face of Dr. Roberts, my ob-gyn. An incredibly kind man with a soft voice and demeanor, he always treated me with great care and respect.

When he walked into my hospital room a few hours after I gave birth, the concern on his face was painfully vivid. My heart shattered when I realized for the first time the true gravity of the situation. I could hardly breathe. My chest seemed to implode from sheer grief. Dr. Roberts sat beside me on the bed and held my hand as I cried, promising to do everything possible to search for answers to Raegan's rare birth defect. Our daughter had a condition called microcephaly, an extremely small head and brain. He would go back over every test to see if we'd missed something along the way.

It's difficult to look back at that time in my life and remember anything but what a tremendous shock Raegan's birth was to my system—physically, mentally, and emotionally. I was a wreck, shaking uncontrollably and sobbing. Spiritually, I felt vacant and abandoned. I remember thinking that this wasn't supposed to happen; every positive expectation of our child's lifetime flashed in our minds like scenes in a movie, haunting us. The many experiences I held dear in my life and thought integral to being a woman would not be a part of Raegan's future—skipping rope, going to college, being a bride. I cried for her, and I cried for me. Mark stayed quiet and seemed to be trying to soak it all in.

"It's doubtful she'll survive, and if she does she'll never be more than an infant. You need to face the fact that your daughter will, at best, be severely retarded with profound medical problems," said one doctor in a matter-of-fact tone.

Each day brought new concerns and more opinions from doctors we'd never met. I remember one particular young pediatrician who was tactfully honest, but hopeful: "No two children are alike. It's hard for us to know so early on," she said. "Kids have a way of surprising you in ways you could never imagine. We need to wait and see."

Because of the overwhelming amount of medical information being shared with us every day, we felt in many ways we'd missed out on experiencing the miracle of Raegan's birth, the joy of her presence entering our lives. Yet when we held her in our arms, everything seemed just fine, as she exuded a peaceful, loving vibe. I called her AngelBaby from the first moment I saw her, as if she'd introduced herself with those words. The name fit, and it is the term of endearment I still use. I would softly sing to Raegan, trying to reassure her and myself:

Sweet little angel, my darling little angel,
Mommy's here, so do not fear,
We can face anything.

The words of the little song flowed from my heart to hers and calmed us both. She was so tiny and new, with a sweet smell of Heaven. Dark hair framed her fragile face like a picture, inviting me to gaze into her captivating blue eyes. A narrow plastic feeding tube went through her nose to her stomach, because the doctors believed she couldn't suck and swallow. Her little fingers curled around my thumb as she lay nestled in my arms. Other than having an extremely small head, she looked and acted much like any other newborn. And our sweet, darling Raegan was about to make herself heard.

It was New Year's Eve, 1999, and the world was abuzz with the Y2K computer issue and whether or not electronics would work after the clock struck twelve. Champagne flowed all around the world in tribute to the century gone by and the new one soon to begin. Raegan had been born the day before and was not expected to live beyond a week or a month at best. The maternity ward was incredibly busy, and we stayed in a private room at the end of a long hallway, trying to cope with all of it. The doctors insisted Raegan spend the night in the hospital nursery so Mark and I could try to get some much needed sleep. Neither of us had closed our eyes in days, and it was rapidly catching up. I accepted a sleeping pill and wearily watched a broadcast of the fireworks over Paris on television until I fell asleep. Mark attempted to rest on a sofa a few feet away. We would not be welcoming the year with a toast or a song.

I heard my baby crying and immediately jumped out of bed, my heart racing. The glowing clock face on the wall showed it was after 2 AM. Eager to be a responsive, caring mother, I peered around and tried to focus in the dark room. Mark was still asleep on the worn plaid couch. Where was the baby? Where was I? Was I dreaming? Was I still pregnant? My heart sank with the sudden realization that Raegan was in the nursery down the hall. The events of the past two days flooded into my mind. I knew I must've heard the baby in the next room crying, not my Angel-Baby. Tears filled my eyes, and I collapsed back on the bed, exhausted and grief stricken.

Just then the door opened, and the sound of a crying baby grew louder. To my surprise, a young nurse wearing a *Happy New Year* tiara came in, cradling Raegan in her arms. She whispered, "Your baby pulled her feeding tube out of her nose and was able to drink from a bottle on her own. She won't stop crying for me. Do you want to give it a try?"

I reached out for Raegan and the tiny bottle, my hands trembling and eyes wide. Mark crawled to the side of the bed with a hesitant, hopeful smile. Raegan quieted immediately and began drinking from the bottle. My heart leaped with intense joy, tears rolling down my face as I watched her take deep gulps of milk. I took a long, slow, deep breath for the first time in days, her essence lifting me in grace and hope. The Divine message she exuded was clear and strong, penetrating through to my being: "Please be strong, Mommy. I need you to help me. It's going to be okay."

Mark and I looked at each other and knew everything had changed for us in one brief, brilliant moment. He sensed the same vibes from our darling girl and knew Daddy was being called to duty. Raegan Aria was on the scene, telling us she was willing to work, but we needed to get over our pain and help her.

Mark and I cried and laughed while feeding and kissing her. We admired her lovely face, toes, and hands, as if seeing them for the first time. Her little sounds soothed our tired ears and quieted our fears. She soon fell asleep and spent the rest of the night cuddling in Mommy's arms. We realized what a blessing this was, in whatever form. Our journey might not be easy, but we now believed we were destined to travel together. That night we learned from our daughter what was truly important: sharing our love with her.

The first sunrise of the new year was a fresh start for us. We had work to do, and we needed to be strong, like Raegan. I ate my breakfast with a newfound appetite and cheerfully danced around the room, holding my precious girl. It seemed easier now to let go of the pain and hopelessness. We had hope, and a beautiful baby calling the shots. We needed to trust her and trust God. From the bathroom, I heard the shower running and Mark whistling a tune as he got ready for the day. I smiled, knowing joy had found its way back into his heart as well. I thanked the Universe for answering my prayer and thanked Raegan for coming into my life. Things were going to be all right, no matter what happened. No matter how much time we had together, things were going to be all right. The earth steadied under my feet as Divine grace replaced fear.

My mom came in about an hour later and immediately felt the change in atmosphere. A new wind had blown in overnight and chased the dark clouds away. I'm an only child, so my mother and I are extremely close and have seen each other through some amazingly difficult times. My first teacher of the intuitive arts, she taught this skill through simple demonstration. Like her mother before her, she trusted her radar and always seemed to know when an issue was looming on the horizon. Mom had spent the past few days slowly dying with us. Now, without a word between us, she knew we'd turned a corner. She would join us in living again.

When we told her about our night and Raegan's turn of events, she took responsibility to pass the word to our family and friends. We now focused on the positive. We would celebrate the birth of Raegan Aria.

PERFECTION IN THE CHAOS

Mark and I will never be the same after this experience, and for that we are grateful. Our lives have changed for the better, as we find perfection in the chaos. We survived the earthquake and no longer hide when a tremor threatens. Honestly, I can't even remember what I thought was important before Raegan's birth. I know I'm more spiritual, caring, honest, patient, and resourceful. I don't get bogged down by issues like money, status, and petty arguments. I was one of those people who sweated the details and tried to take responsibility for everyone and everything. Now I know I have to care for myself first in order to be strong for my family.

I try not to waste energy worrying about details out of my control, like the weather or shifts in the earth's crust. I still get upset, cry, and scream, but that helps too. I accept my humanity and try not to deny my emotions; I grow by experiencing them. When our AngelBaby helped us look past our self-doubt and fear to the miracle of her birth, we were able to see our situation as the blessing it is. She triggered the Divine energy deep in our hearts and reminded us of our connection to God.

I share Raegan's story with you because she represents the heart of every child I've ever had the joy to encounter. If you are reading this as a parent of a medically fragile child, you will find not only a beautiful reflection of your own life but also numerous techniques to assist you and your child on the path to wellness. If you are reading this as the parent of a challenging child, one who tests your emotional boundaries or just pushes your buttons, you will discover methods that promote relaxation, peaceful communication, and family unity. And if you are the parent, teacher, or caregiver of a child free from medical or emotional issues, you will explore a vast array of tools that open the intuitive hearts of us all, leading to a life of deep awareness and grace. We have all been blessed with innate intuitive parenting abilities. We only need to make the choice to access this sacred part of ourselves. Come along with me and discover how this amazing form of intuition works within you.

THE WISDOM OF CHILDREN

The powerless in our world do hold great power.
The weak do confound the mighty.
—CHRISTOPHER DE VINCK, *THE POWER OF THE POWERLESS*

In my ongoing work as a holistic practitioner and intuitive consultant, I have been delighted to discover how all children effortlessly rely on their subtle energy system to communicate. I cannot do a section on the energetic strengths of children without telling you about Raegan's friend, Connor. This extraordinary young man was only a few years old when he first introduced his mother, Mary, and me. A local television station featured a human-interest story on Raegan and related medical research. According to Connor's mother, when Raegan appeared on the screen during the news story, Connor started saying, "Baby, baby . . . look, Mommy!" After his relentless urgings, she stopped what she was doing to watch the segment. By this time, little Connor had moved to the screen, touching it and calling out to Raegan as if she was an old friend. In an email to me, she reported he'd never before acted that way, though he'd seen countless images of children on television. We began corresponding by phone and email and discovered our families had much in common, including sharing a few medical specialists. It turned out I also knew her father, a beloved postal worker in my hometown.

Our friendship blossomed over the years, yet with our busy families, it was often difficult to get together. One morning I received a phone call from Mary. It was sort of funny she called, because I was getting ready to phone her to invite her and Connor to visit us that day. I explained we were checking in to a hotel not far from where they lived to attend a formal party that evening. My mom was going to watch Raegan in the hotel room while we attended a reception downstairs in the ballroom. If she and Connor came to the hotel, we'd have several hours to hang out and visit before Mark arrived from work.

"Are you kidding?" she asked. "I can't *believe* this. When Connor woke up this morning, he told me he was ready to go to the hotel! I told him we weren't going away on vacation, and he just laughed at me and said, 'You'll see!'"

Needless to say, we had a lovely time together visiting at the hotel. How was Connor able to know about these plans ahead of time? His intuitive energy system knew before the words were spoken. Energetically, the plans were already out there. With no hesitation or reservations holding him back, he was able to absorb the information and make use of it. I believe children can tap in to sources we limit with our egos, judgments, and attachments to the material world. Could it be that Raegan and Connor "talked" to each other before Mary and I got around to it? Perhaps he saw it in his mind's eye or as a whisper in his little ear. The important point is: we all get this kind of information when we're open to it.

Scientific research on energy medicine, telepathy, and intuition is expanding and gaining greater credibility in conventional circles. Compelling evidence suggests the brain and heart operate in conjunction to receive, process, and decode intuitive information. This is now considered a complete body process involving a number of human systems, and it further indicates how knowledge about future events emanates from an energy field. I'll delve further into the specific research behind energy medicine in the next few chapters. It's exciting to imagine a future in which this natural ability is nurtured, developed, and celebrated for the enrichment of all.

IT'S YOUR TURN

The more people have studied different methods of bringing up children, the more they have come to the conclusion that what good mothers and fathers instinctively feel like doing for their babies is the best after all.
—BENJAMIN SPOCK, DR. SPOCK'S BABY AND CHILD CARE

Now I'd like to get you started on the HeartGlow intuitive parenting development process. Our ultimate goal for the information, exercises, and activities in this book is to help you become an intuitive energy expert—someone who relies on your subtle energy system to live an extraordinary, energetic life, for both yourself and your family. With this heightened knowledge and skill, you will become an exceptional intuitive parent and be able to

- Hold a greater understanding of yourself and others
- Enrich your family's health in mind, body, and spirit
- Learn techniques to address pain, anxiety, stress, and seizures
- Improve sleep patterns, tackle behavioral issues, and bond with your child
- Rely on your intuitive heart for communication enhancement and healing
- Increase your overall quality of life by embracing your connection to the Divine

I'd like you to select a journal or notebook to use during your HeartGlow intuitive parenting exploration. Please choose whatever feels right for you—a three-ring-binder, a steno pad, or a beautiful book. You'll need many blank pages where you can write, draw, laugh, scream, cry, and basically connect with your soul. I've saved my numerous journals over the years and love going back to revisit the pages. Reliving the initial stages of your HeartGlow journey will help you see how far you've come in growth and understanding. Each person should have her own journal; don't share with someone else. If you're exploring your relationship with multiple children, be sure to look at each relationship individually.

Now get out there to find your journal and writing implements. We all know it can be a blast shopping for office supplies, so have fun with it. Meet me back here when you're ready.

HEARTGLOW EXERCISES

Each chapter in this book will provide two formal exercises that give you a chance to stretch your intuitive parenting muscle. You'll have greater success in the HeartGlow development process if you carry out the exercises as written. These techniques are only beneficial when used on a regular basis. I also encourage you to take detailed notes and reflect on other parts of the chapter that resonate with you. The HeartGlow Hints at the end of each chapter provide another opportunity for you to discover your glowing heart.

EXERCISE 1: HEARTGLOW JOURNALING

Welcome to your first exercise of HeartGlow Journaling. In your HeartGlow journal, please, in all love and honesty, finish the following statements:

1. I first felt my intuition when . . .

2. I want to help myself by . . .

3. I want to help my child by . . .

4. My doubts and fears about why this might not work are . . .

5. I feel my child is here to teach me . . .

6. I am here to teach my child . . .

7. This is what I admire most about myself . . .

8. This is what I admire most about my child . . .

9. I believe God is . . .

10. I am interested in HeartGlow because . . .

Your answers are your own. There is no right or wrong way to complete the information. Please take your time and answer from the deepest part of yourself with total honesty. If you become anxious, then put the work down and revisit the task when you are feeling more balanced and comfortable.

EXERCISE 2: EXPANSIVE VISUALIZATION
SEE YOUR CHILD'S UNLIMITED POSSIBILITIES

In this exercise, you're going to take a little trip with your child's energy. You will journey together to places you have never been before, exploring little-known corners of our world and even galaxies beyond. To prepare for this excursion, I'd like you to go to a place in your home where you can be alone for twenty minutes. This could be in your bedroom, an office, or even the bathtub. I know private places are hard to come by in a busy family, but consider this a small step in changing your ingrained patterns and behaviors. You need to start making time for your own explorations of uncharted territory. You're worth it!

You may use a soothing instrumental CD in the background if you find it helps you achieve a more tranquil state. Get yourself into a relaxed position and close your eyes. Take a few deep breaths through your nose and exhale from your mouth. Now I would like you to visualize your child. Project a beautiful picture of your child into your mind's eye with as many details as you can bring forth. Clearly imagine their physical being: hair color, facial features, and maybe a favorite outfit. Think how much you love him. Send love. Send hugs and kisses. Send light and grace. Now allow your child to take you on a flying journey. Hold his hand and soar into the sky together, with your child slightly in the lead. Both of you are relaxed, comfortable, and excited about this adventure with no fear or anxiety holding you back. It is thrilling to be doing this together. Where do you go? What do you see? Are you able to distinguish any particular colors or places? Do you hear sounds? Is anyone else there? Visualize this magical journey with your child. Let your spirit soar high above any concerns or worries you may have in day-to-day life. Be open to anything that comes before you and allow your creativity to blossom. There are no limits to the places you can go on this flight of mystic whimsy.

Spend as long as you wish soaring through the air with your child. You are both exuberant and happy to be together. Take the time to explore new vistas and peek into hidden nooks and hollows. Celebrate the surprises around each corner and know you are blessed to be seeing them. When you naturally feel yourself returning home, thank your child for his love, time, and energy. Embrace him with a warm hug and plan to do it again, to discover distant horizons together. When you return to your body (yes, you did leave for a bit), give yourself a few moments and then write your reflections of the flight in your journal. Try to recall the details: sights, sounds, tastes, textures, and smells. Did you receive messages from your child or anyone else? How did you feel? Did you learn anything about yourself or about your child? Write down whatever comes to your heart and mind about this experience. This is only the beginning of your soul dialogue, so relax and don't fear doing it incorrectly. We all do things differently, and your way is what is right for you at this time.

Don't be surprised if your child brings you to a departed loved one with whom he enjoys spending time in the heavens. All energy is eternal and can be accessed when we are in the proper state. Our soul bodies are not limited by time or physicality. Please repeat this exercise as often as you like. Raegan and I go on flights together on a regular basis, and I continually learn new things about her. I often go into this visualization just before falling asleep for the night and have gone on to have incredible dreams, leading to tremendous insights. Where will you go when you allow your feet to leave the ground?

SUMMARY OF KEY POINTS

Children intuitively draw upon the Divine energy source and bring forth awareness to those willing to listen with a loving heart. Parents can employ their intuitive hearts, their HeartGlow, as a commanding instrument in orchestrating their family's needs. HeartGlow methods bridge scientific knowledge of energy medicine with holistic, traditional, and spiritual approaches.

Your life can change for the better when you find perfection in chaos. Children trigger the Divine energy deep in our hearts and remind us of our connection to God. The energy inherent in parent-child relationships plays a crucial role in communication and healing. Parents need to see relationships with their children in a new light, with increased awareness and depth. Learning to acknowledge children as soul beings with vast innate knowledge to share is the key to greater joy in life.

You can develop a greater energy connection with your child and dramatically improve the quality of life for your family. Children effortlessly rely on their subtle energy system to communicate. Children can tap in to sources we often limit due to our egos, judgments, and attachment to the material world. Life takes on a new dimension when feeling the glow of an intuitive heart.

HeartGlow Hints for Intuitive Parenting

- Listen to your children with your heart, not only your ears.
- Take time to reflect back to your child's birth. What did you notice or sense before or during their birth?
- Be willing to change your attachment to your perceptions in life. Can you see things differently?
- Slow down. Take a deep breath. Discover the calm within.
- See your children as the individual, vibrant souls they are. Are you limiting them with labels?

2

The Essence of HeartGlow

Your daily life is your temple and your religion.
Whenever you enter into it take with you your all.

KAHLIL GIBRAN, *THE PROPHET*

The essence of intuitive parenting is learning how to live with an open, intuitive heart. But what does this mean, and how do you do it? I can tell you, in the shadow of those first few days after Raegan's birth, this was not the first question on my mind. But gently, she taught me how to slow down, listen, and pay attention to my inner wisdom, guiding me through several harrowing situations with the help of this tremendous bond. You may be thinking, "How can I slow down when this toddler is keeping me on my feet all day? When this newborn is keeping me up all night! I barely have time for a minute to myself!" I'll show you the way, and you'll also learn how essential it is to have some quiet time to yourself. So, do take advantage of your spouse's offer to help out or of a family member's loving arms to hold the baby. Enjoy those quiet moments of stillness to recharge your batteries and connect to your own intuitive heart.

For each and every one of us, there is a place deep within that is sacred. This is the quiet voice of intuition that calls to us, the voice of our souls; scholars and philosophers throughout history have called it our higher self. In the Hindu tradition, it is the *Atman*: our individual spiritual essence. For Christians, it is the Holy Spirit. In other religious traditions, this special, sacred voice represents our connection with God, the Absolute, or the Supreme Being for each different system of belief. Regardless of which term you feel comfortable using, think of this voice as your conduit to a higher source of information that can guide and inform you, if you take the time to listen.

I believe we all have the ability to connect with this Source, and with each other, by utilizing our natural energy. Science and spirituality meet as we begin understanding the amazing interactive talents of our hearts, minds, and bodies. Regardless of your chosen religion or spiritual path, take comfort in knowing that when we are at one with God, we are all one.

HeartGlow is our conscious awareness of Divine energy radiating from our core, when our essence (or God light) emits its unique glow out to the receptive, loving Universe and receives guidance, love, and support in return. When you live your life with a glowing heart, you are making a choice to access and flow with Divine energy. So think of your journey to intuitive parenting as a way of life—a journey into a new way of being. To access your HeartGlow at this very moment, simply take a deep breath and say the word "Love." Feel warmth and power begin to emanate from the center of your chest as the glowing embers deep inside you begin stirring from the word.

For those of you reading who are thinking, "OK, this is a little outside of my realm of experience," think of it this way: your five physical senses combine to inform you about your world, but do you notice them working? In the same way, you've possibly experienced some kind of sudden understanding—a warning, an insight, or even a decision to choose one action over another. Looking at intuitive parenting from a slightly more analytical perspective, it can be thought of as a form of deep insight, a heightened perception of the world around you.

Whichever way you look at it, the information throughout this book is designed to help you discover your own Divine inner guidance system—your HeartGlow—and to use that glowing heart to be a successful and loving intuitive parent. By opening your mind to the possibilities, you will be able to develop skills, heighten your sensitivities and—making use of your loving connections to enhance communication—utilize energy healing, and restore balance for your family. By embracing your inner wisdom, you pave the way to a new energetic realm and the blissful life of intuitive parenting.

OUR SUBTLE ENERGY SYSTEM

We've been throwing the word around, now let's clearly define it. *Energy* is our great power within, the Divine Life Force—Spirit flowing magnificently through us, in us, and around us. Energy is our capacity to connect with and be part of the Higher Consciousness on all levels of existence. It is known throughout the world by many names, such as Prana, Qi, Chi, Ki, and the Universal Life Force.

Your individual subtle energy system interacts with and processes universal energy. Just as we have physical bodies that enable us to relate to the physical world, we have an energetic body to handle energy information. Most energy practitioners, whether they come from an Eastern, yogic, holistic, or psychological point of view, agree the human energy system has three primary subsystems: an energy field, energy centers, and energy pathways.

Each of these is known by a number of different names, according to the particular culture or belief system, as this chart displays:

General	Yogic	Chinese/ Eastern	Energy Medicine
Energy	Prana	Qi, Chi, Ki	Vitality, Life Force
Energy Field	Aura	Wei Chi	Reservoirs, Biofield
Energy Centers	Chakras	Acu-points	Transformers
Energy Pathway	Nadis	Meridians	Channels

Many philosophies, theories, and schools of thought on the subtle energy system set hard-and-fast rules and practices on how it should be interpreted based on their beliefs. I choose to have an eclectic and expansive view of this crucial system. By leaving the heart and mind open to other perspectives, we do not limit the possibilities. We all perceive the Universe differently, so it makes sense to me that none of us sees or feels things exactly the same way. A significant number of my client families work outside of traditional parameters. For example, you can't set color restrictions when a member of your family is blind or doesn't have the intellectual capacity to do something in a regimented, cerebral way. My own daughter is cortically blind, nonverbal, and considered by the medical establishment to be "profoundly mentally retarded." If we operated under strict confines, we'd miss out on the boundless power of energy transformation. The idea is to move creatively and openly into a new dimension of yourself and others. Raegan is a beautiful demonstration that we have no limits when dancing with the Divine.

Our unique internal system will guide each of us on the path we need to take. So when someone says you're wrong for sending radiant pink light for love instead of green or blue, simply thank them for their opinion and know your intuition has guided you in the direction you needed to go. Your pure intention is truly what matters. The dogma of fixed belief is by far more cumbersome to carry than the light in your own heart.

The guidelines I present here are merely that: guidelines. May this initial structure ignite your quest for knowledge and be the launching pad for your flight into the energetic realms.

THE HUMAN ENERGY FIELD: OUR COAT OF MANY COLORS

The human energy field, also known as the aura or biofield, encompasses all living things and can provide clues to the health and overall well-being of a person or thing. Trees, animals, people, and even insects all have their own energetic fields. Those of us who use our heightened sense of perception can detect the aura and the subtle information it contains. Many people who are energy sensitive can visually perceive auras with their eyes, while others sense them through a more intuitive process, such as the mind's eye. Think of the biofield as a multidimensional radiant pool of energy that envelops you and can extend dozens of feet beyond your body in a large oval or egg shape.

Auras appear in the art and philosophy of a number of world cultures, including Indian, Chinese, and Egyptian. In the small Christian church I attended as a child, a large portrait of Jesus hung in the sanctuary with a beautiful golden aura surrounding his head and praying hands. I remember instinctually knowing the golden light meant you were with God. In working with Heart-Glow families, aura cleansing is an essential step in clearing stagnant energy that has been trapped by fear, anxiety, and other intense emotions.

ENERGY CENTERS: THE REAL FAMILY JEWELS

Energy centers, also commonly referred to as chakras, are the central points of energy activity in our bodies and subtle energy systems. They are responsible for decoding, exploring, and processing the life force energy we encounter. I like to think of these vital centers as beautiful jewels embedded in our energetic bodies. Each of them spins, glows, and pulsates with intense colors. Children instinctively relate to the idea of having these vibrant treasures within them and enjoy making the crystals at the centers of their palms shine and vibrate.

Although there are hundreds of energy centers in our body, most chakra authorities refer to the seven major centers, which run vertically along our spine from our head to our tail. Science and technology are beginning to catch up with ancient philosophy as devices are being developed that pinpoint the exact location of the energy centers within our body. The chart on the next page shows the location of major energy points within our bodies and their corresponding attributes.

ENERGY PATHWAYS: GOING WITH THE FLOW

Energy pathways, also referred to as *nadis,* or meridians, are the channels by which energies flow within our subtle energy system. Consider these pathways as complex, extensive, and intricate as the physical body's circulatory or nervous system. In fact, these channels form a web that connects and communicates with the

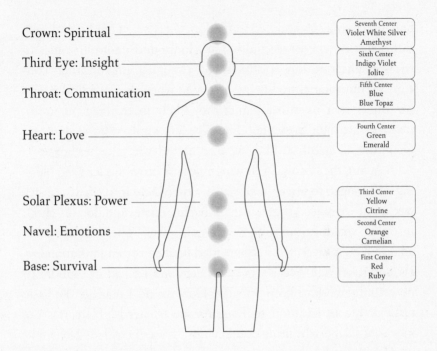

Crown: Spiritual — Seventh Center / Violet White Silver / Amethyst

Third Eye: Insight — Sixth Center / Indigo Violet / Iolite

Throat: Communication — Fifth Center / Blue / Blue Topaz

Heart: Love — Fourth Center / Green / Emerald

Solar Plexus: Power — Third Center / Yellow / Citrine

Navel: Emotions — Second Center / Orange / Carnelian

Base: Survival — First Center / Red / Ruby

hundreds of energy centers within us, distributing subtle energy signals to all major systems and organs of our physical body.

These pathways are not nerves, but rather, they are thought to be hollow portals for the free stream of consciousness. Nadis, from the root *nad* in Sanskrit, translates to "channel" or "flow." Just as the energy of electricity moves through intricate circuits, our vital force energy flows through every part of our body via these pathways. According to the Upanishads, ancient Hindu texts, there are thought to be nearly one hundred thousand channels through which our energy travels within our subtle energy system.

THE VOICES BEGIN

The days following Raegan's birth were challenging but seemed to grow lighter as we shifted our perspective. Astonished by our daughter's strength and determination, we cheered her on and took our victories where we could. The gloom-and-doom attitudes of the specialists no longer affected us, though I am sure their concern for our mental well-being increased when their medical jargon no longer sent us into a panic; they likely interpreted our calm, peaceful attitude as denial. But Raegan's vitals were strong and beginning to stabilize. They were going to let us take her home.

Leaving the hospital following Raegan's birth was a mixed blessing. We longed to leave the box-like room where we'd spent nearly a week, but we missed the security of having nurses and doctors check in on us, making sure things were going well. These experienced, educated people verified Raegan's food intake, oxygen saturation levels, and heart rate. Meals were provided, and we had no laundry to do or housework to keep up with. How would I manage the basic tasks of life in addition to Raegan's special needs? Here was the moment I'd been waiting for, yet now I was petrified. My mind raced with fearful thoughts of inadequacy. What if she had a seizure or started choking? Would I know if she was in trouble?

I methodically packed our bags in preparation for departure. January is a frightfully cold month in Maine, and I wanted to make sure Raegan was cozy for the twenty-minute ride home. The bunting I'd selected from my shower gifts was no longer appropriate, as it was much too large for her six-pound frame. The hood seemed immense around her tiny head. I opted for another outfit and the little hat the hospital provided, lovingly crocheted by an unknown senior citizen. It fit just right and more than likely had been intended for a preemie. The cap was made of the softest yarn imaginable in a lovely mix of pastel green, yellow, and white. Mark had already left to bring our car around to the exit. I was wearing real clothes for the first time since we'd arrived, abandoning hospital attire for stretch pants and a warm sweater. I was surprised at how loosely everything fit. Several long days of not eating had left me within only a few pounds of my pre-pregnancy weight. I laughed at myself for thinking of that as a positive; I was trying to be optimistic whenever I could.

Overall, Raegan was doing well. After her initial bottle-feeding on New Year's Eve, she'd been able to maintain that skill, and we were working on breastfeeding. My intention had always been to breastfeed, but it was posing a bit of a struggle for us. Dr. Hobbs, our pediatrician, came into our room during one of our lactation attempts when Raegan and I were both in tears from frustration. Giving me a wink, she said, "Don't rush yourself. Let's be thankful for what we have." I smiled gratefully in agreement.

We had met Dr. Hobbs at an expectant parents' night at the hospital a month before my delivery date, and I was immediately impressed by her knowledge, openness, and exuberance. She had a glow about her, which appealed to me. Looking back from an energy perspective, I now realize this was one of the first clear indications I was receiving help from a higher source. More signs would come.

As we drove home cautiously on the icy streets, I sat in back with Raegan so I could watch her every breath. Mark was thrilled about leaving the hospital. He'd taken a few breaks from the tense atmosphere to run errands and follow up on household responsibilities, but now we were all free. "I am taking my girls home," he announced triumphantly. "The cats are going to go crazy when they see you." My cats Casey and Puffy had been my best buddies for over ten years, and I'd honed my mothering skills on them. Now I was concerned about how they'd react to Raegan.

We turned the final corner onto our street, then into the driveway. The house looked exactly the same, a conservative light green ranch home with a large blue spruce in front. I don't know why I thought it would look different. It was comforting to see things had stayed the same, even though I had changed.

Mark was right. The cats swarmed around my legs as I stepped through the doorway, meowing their hellos. I took my coat off and sat down with them while Mark brought Raegan from the van. Animals exude unconditional love and understanding. The friendly purrs calmed me, welcoming me back to my life.

"Here's the AngelBaby," Mark said as he carried Raegan in, gently placing her in my arms and kissing her on the forehead. I introduced her to the cats by holding her close to their curious noses. To my surprise, both cats jumped onto the couch on either side of us and lay against me like purring bookends. They sweetly watched Raegan and began to soak up her radiance. No fear. No snarls. No jealousy. Simply acceptance. After a few moments, I got up to look around the house, handing Raegan to Mark so I could get a few things done. The cats remained by her side. They knew she was something special, and they were now officially on angel duty.

Our home looked incredibly cheerful, filled with flowers, balloons, and stuffed animals sent by family, friends, and co-workers. The fragrance of blossoms filled every corner and brought a smile to my face. The house wasn't exactly as we left it after rushing out the door in active labor. Everything was much better. I opened the fridge, preparing to make a list of the numerous grocery items we would need to re-establish our routine. But I was dumbfounded as I surveyed the shelves: they were loaded with casseroles, soups, and entire meals, all marked with labels and notes of encouragement from our friends. I looked into a few grocery bags on the counter and found pastries, cookies, cereal, paper plates, and cups. I wandered through the house in amazement, feeling as though someone had waved a magic wand. Every room was spotless—floors vacuumed, laundry folded, and not a speck of dust in sight. My "sisters" had been here and were clearly bent on taking care of us. Warms tears of appreciation slid down my cheeks.

Though I have no biological sisters, spiritually I am a sister to some of the best women in the world. When my heart was breaking in the hospital, they enveloped me with their loving, nurturing souls. They each cried with me and for me. This circle of friends has faced the fires of divorce, adultery, death, and betrayal. We've celebrated engagements, marriages, pregnancies, and now, a not-so-traditional birth. Now they were providing a foundation when I didn't have a leg to stand on, literally putting food in my mouth and giving strength to my system. I wouldn't have survived those first few weeks without their support. I know that for certain. Their presence was my greatest gift.

Raegan adjusted well to life at home. She seemed extremely comfortable and was truly thriving. I wasn't doing too badly in the new mother role. Like most new moms, I wasn't getting much sleep and looked horrible, with dark circles and constant bed head. Mark and I took turns pacing the floor at 2 AM trying to calm our screaming baby. I became quite familiar with late night television. Raegan and I were able to bond in a traditional way and, without the hospital equipment around us, we didn't have constant reminders of her disabilities. Most nights I fell asleep on the couch, sitting up with her lying on my chest.

One late night as we sat quietly in the darkened living room, I began to panic. This had occurred periodically before—a sensation that a forest was closing in around me. Hungry tree roots grabbed at my ankles, while their limbs and shadowy foliage blocked my view of the sky and path ahead. This forest of fear grew increasingly dark and dense, and my mind raced with a million disorganized thoughts. How would we get by? What would I do about my job? What if Raegan died? My heart raced, and tears streamed down my face. I rose and paced the floor, my chest getting tighter and tighter. I was ramping myself up into a panic attack, anxious thoughts dragging me into a deep chasm of despair. The room began to pulse and swirl around me as I collapsed back onto the couch in a daze.

Through half-open eyes, I saw two figures move toward me. One of them took Raegan out of my arms, cradling her, whispering soft lullabies. The other sat beside me, stroking my face and hair. "*Feel the light inside you. Let it guide you,*" she said. "*Your daughter is not afraid and feels confident in your care. You chose this. She chose this. We will be here to help you.*"

These serene figures were hard to distinguish in the dark room. They weren't exactly people and seemed to change shape, color, and size right in front of me. The harder I tried to see them with my eyes, the fainter they became. "Don't go!" I called as I startled awake.

Raegan was sleeping tenderly on my chest, and no one else was in the room. Looking around, I felt recognition, as though I'd just visited with my great-grandmother who died when I was a child. "Nana," I cried aloud. "Please come back!" Taking a deep breath, I placed Raegan into her crib and went to bed. Ten hours later, I awoke. We had both slept soundly for the first time since coming home.

During breakfast, I tried to wrap my brain around what had happened. How could it be my Nana? It didn't look like her; it just felt like her. I thought back to our special snack sessions of crackers-n-milk when I was little, barely able to sit on a chair by myself. I could clearly remember her face smiling at me as I scooped up the mush with my spoon. My heart soared as I recognized the resonance of her love. It was Nana. Some things you need to wrap your heart around to know.

Although my Nana didn't come back for another visit, I began to "hear" from others. One night while asleep in my bed, I heard "*Deb!*"

"What?" I asked of Mark, who was lying beside me. There was no reply, as he was sound asleep.

"*Deb, now!*" the voice insisted. I abruptly sat up, trying to figure out what was going on and whether or not I was dreaming. My body tensed. "Raegan needs me," I whispered. I bounded from my bed and ran to her. My daughter's arm was dangling from under the bumper pad of her crib. She was pinned between the rails, a blanket covering her entire body and face.

"Oh my God!" I cried as I grabbed for her, removing her arm from the slatted side and lifting her up to me. She was perfectly fine and still sleeping soundly. "Thank you … thank you … thank you for watching over us," I said, not sure who or what I was thanking: my ancestors, or maybe angels? It didn't matter to me; I was just glad someone was there.

FINDING OUR FOOTING

I so often wished we had more information to share with friends and family, but much was still unknown. We finally had a diagnosis from Raegan's brain MRI: microlissencephaly with agenesis of the corpus callosum. We had no idea what that meant—or the true implications for our life. Basically, Raegan had a rare birth defect that left her brain abnormally small and malformed. She was expected to live two weeks but had already blown past that prognosis. We opted to take things bit by bit; even one day at a time was too much.

Every part of my body ached to let go of my prior life and not worry about returning to work. I enjoyed the bonding time with Raegan, getting to know her little coos and gestures. My practical side knew we had bills to pay and we couldn't survive without my salary. With my maternity leave half over, I had no idea what we were going to do. The plans we'd made for child care had long since fallen apart. "I'm not really equipped to handle special-needs children," the caretaker said. "I have to think about my own kids and how this would affect them. It's not really fair to them if I spend all my time on one child. I'm sorry."

Yet, these issues began to fade. Whenever my mind began racing with worry, I recalled the advice to feel the light inside me. Recognizing that eternal glow of peace in my heart made me feel centered, supported, and less afraid.

Returning to my job after the maternity leave was used up didn't work out, even though I attempted to shift to a part-time, home-based office. I discovered that after all we'd been through, I no longer had the stamina or the desire to do what I used to do or be who I used to be. My perception of the world had changed drastically, and I didn't have it in me to be corporate anymore. That chapter of my life had come to an end.

We did find a way to get by financially, and I surprised our friends and family by turning in my briefcase for an apron. I went back to the profession that sustained us during my college years: waitressing. Others thought I was crazy to leave behind everything I'd worked for at the insurance company, but I felt relieved to let go of those responsibilities. I could spend my days with Raegan and then leave for the restaurant when Mark arrived home. We were literally exchanging kisses and keys in the driveway so our daughter would always have a parent in charge of her care. I was usually home before midnight and could take over the late night feeding and let Mark go to bed. We operated on little sleep, but the benefit of quality time far outweighed any inconvenience.

The time seemed to fly past, and Raegan was nearly a year old. We were amazed by the sheer joy she exuded and thankful for her stable health. Carol, a home health aide, began assisting me a few hours each day with Raegan's care. An experienced mother and grandmother, she had a calming effect on all of us. Therapists made weekly visits to aid Raegan's development. My days took on the new purpose of helping my child not merely survive but flourish. Slowly, I felt my way through the situation and redefined my place in the world. I could see hints of light gleaming in the dark, dense forest. My footing grew more stable on the cool, damp earth. The path was less encumbered by brambles and fallen trees. I still felt afraid at times but also impressed by the beauty along the trail. Exquisite blossoms of love, understanding, and friendship were guiding me to Raegan and to my spiritual self. I could feel the energy inside me swirling like a cyclone and knew I was on the verge of something incredible.

When I think back to those first few months of Raegan's life, I can clearly see how much she was reaching out to me with her heart. The clues I was receiving along the way greatly assisted with her daily care. I now also realize how my own internal guidance system was becoming heightened to adapt to the needs and circumstances of my life. Following my inner compass and moving beyond fear, I was able to make decisions about work, home, and relationships that greatly benefited my family.

Every bump, scrape, and cry of a child turns a parent's physical senses on high alert. It is ingrained in us to react to events as they unfold before our eyes. Through engaging your intuitive parenting senses, you can access the energy of an event and intervene even before a bandage is required. Just as I do, you will learn to trust your intuition as a practical tool in a busy household.

ENERGY COMMUNICATION: INTUITION IS CHANNELING

When we think about caring for our families, communication from sources outside our physical perception isn't usually on the list of related topics. Food, clothing, shelter, and even emotional needs such as self-esteem, respect, and love usually take most of our energy and attention. We're accustomed to dealing with what we can see with our eyes and touch with our hands. Yet, out-of-this-world information channeled from mysterious sources can be an invaluable aid to parents. Intuitive insight can provide clues for fast action or can bring forth information to develop an appropriate healing protocol in a chronic situation. Divine guidance comes to all of us openly and freely; we must use energy expertise to decipher the message being delivered.

Author Jon Klimo defines channeling as the "ability to act as a vehicle for thoughts, images, feelings, and information coming from a source that is beyond the individual's self and from beyond ordinary reality."[1] Channeling encompasses a number of methods and fields of practice, including ESP, mediumship, intuition, clairvoyance, and telepathy. The title isn't important. The common thread among all these methods is Divine energy at the heart of the communication. The energy is delivered to the physical plane through different methods and channels. Like human radios, we are able to receive the signals when we tune to the proper frequency.

Most people relate to the concept of channeling through the softer term *intuition*. We may be comfortable with the concept of gaining innate knowledge, a hunch, or a strong suspicion about something, yet we're fearful when the information is more than casual. Knowing the next song on the radio before it plays or predicting who'll win a baseball game is fun. These little hunches can apply to a variety of subjects, including business matters, family relationships, financial investments, and even medical issues. Take the hint from the Universe and open yourself up to higher knowing. Amazing things happen when you go beyond your comfort zone and develop your psychic senses.

Intuition in action can make a good businessperson great or turn a doctor into a miracle worker. When parents put their intuitive hearts into action, they may save a life. There are no limits. To move beyond the hunch factor, you need to work on it.

The three processes of *clairvoyance*, *clairaudience*, and *clairsentience* play a key role in understanding the nature of HeartGlow and how intuitive guidance works in your body and personal energy field. Anyone willing to tap into his/her own inner wisdom can access the energy of the higher planes—energy that will brilliantly convey messages to you at all times. You need not be a professional psychic or medium to channel universal truth and benefit from the deep awareness of intuition. Appreciating how this information is moving through you is a crucial step on the path of energy ascension.

Clairvoyance (clear seeing) is intuitive information coming to us clearly and concisely through dreams, mental images, and creative insights. We see this information with the mind's eye, like a movie or a symbolic picture. A significant number of HeartGlow parents report messages from angels, spirit guides, or departed loved ones who come to them in their dreams to foretell of upcoming circumstances. I often get visions to interpret after I pose specific questions to the Universe.

Clairaudience (clear hearing) is the ability to hear information from outside sources, almost like a special inner ear. This skill is often associated with mediums and psychics who hear messages from spirit guides or departed loved ones. A lover of music, I discovered early in my work as an intuitive consultant that songs related to a client's particular issue would pop into my head. Spirit creatively uses the distinct language and library of your mind to reach you. The more you know about a variety of topics, the greater chance of successful communication. Many of my students have discovered the true meaning of earlier messages after they deepened their knowledge base.

Clairsentience (clear feeling) is when intuitive information resides in a person's energy field and is then delivered to the conscious mind by a cue from the physical body. A certain twinge in the stomach or lift in the heart upon meeting a new person is the intuitive system's way of communicating valuable information. Or it can also be a sense of just knowing something. Most people recognize this ability to one degree or another. The next time your body begins to communicate a message, take a moment and tap in to its greater meaning.

Scientific research on intuition and channeling is expanding and gaining greater credibility in conventional circles. Published studies by Rollin McCraty and his team of researchers at the Institute of HeartMath reveal compelling evidence that the brain and heart operate in conjunction to receive, process, and decode intuitive information. Based upon their clinical efforts in exploring this occurrence, the researchers propose that intuitive perception is a complete body process involving a number of human systems in which knowledge about future events emanates from an energy field.[2]

As a parent, you can use intuitive skills as a powerful tool in managing your family's unique requirements. As you become more receptive to the subtle clues of inner knowing, you will perceive, interpret, and act on information not accessible by other means. My client Sharon, a mother of a young baby, was amazed at her natural ability to tend to her son's needs before he verbally called to her. Often sensing his desire for food, a specific toy, or even cuddles, she relaxed into the sensations and successfully followed her inner flow. She told me, "I never really knew what they meant by mother's intuition, until I lived it myself." Sharon has continued to develop her intuitive parenting abilities and reaps the benefits. You can too!

HeartGlow Exercises

It's time to put what you've learned about the subtle energy system to practice. Here are two more formal exercises that give you a chance to put your intuitive parenting skills to the test. Remember, to have greater success in the HeartGlow development process, you'll want to carry out the exercises as written and on a regular basis. I know you can do it!

EXERCISE 3: AURA WASH: ENERGY FIELD CLEANSING

Now it's time to learn how to cleanse our auric fields. This is an excellent exercise for you and your family and can be formatted to whatever style works best for you. You might sit in a circle to do the activity together as a family, with everyone's participation, or use your parental skills to wash the aura of a family member while that person is sleeping. When Raegan or I feel under the weather or stressed, I perform an Aura Wash to clear away energy debris that may be contributing to the situation. By cleansing your own personal energy field, you're being responsible and respectful of your energetic self. You're honoring and processing what is yours and releasing what you don't need to hold on to.

The Aura Wash begins with a routine called the HeartGlow Primer, which gets us into a receptive, relaxed state. This is a fantastic starting point for most of our exercises and is also beneficial to do on its own, whenever you need to stop the chaos and reconnect with Source.

To begin the HeartGlow Primer, put yourself into a relaxed state by sitting comfortably in a chair with your back straight and well supported. Take a few deep breaths, inhaling slowly through your nose and exhaling slowly from your mouth. Allow the frustrations of the day to leave you, floating far out of your mind. Relax. Shake loose any body part that's holding tension. Reach up and run your hands through your hair a few times, slightly tugging your hair, as you run your nails across your scalp. Embrace yourself by wrapping both arms snuggly around your body; send yourself love, acceptance, and understanding. Now move your hands and arms to a comfortable position on your lap. Slowly take another deep breath. Say aloud or to yourself: "I am Light. I am Peace. I am Love."

Now, with your mind's eye, envision the auric field around you. See its egg-like shape envelop your body. This field can extend dozens of feet outward in many subtle layers. What does your aura look like? What does it feel like? Do you see colors dancing through it? Are they light or dark? Are the colors fixed or moving? Do you see debris floating around? What does this debris look like? Can you perceive any weaknesses or tears in the fabric of your aura? Do any areas need attention or mending? Take a few moments to feel your perceptions. Be in this moment with them. Know in your heart nothing here can harm you. This is merely another dimension and expression of your life at this moment—a new way of looking at you.

Once you've familiarized yourself with your auric field, begin the wash. Using the powerful, vibrant colors of your energy centers, slowly wash your aura by bathing it in colorful light. One by one, slowly project each color into your auric field, beginning with the first center and working upward: red, orange, yellow, green, blue, indigo, and violet. Do your colors cut sharply like a laser, or slowly float into every curve? How is your creative process doing this exercise? Each of us is different and that is wonderful.

Once you've moved through the spectrum of energy center colors, allow your intuitive self to further wash your aura with its own unique colors. Are they single colors, or do they blend and swirl together? Could they be a specific shade from your past or a hint at something yet to come? What are the colors of your life? All of this is a beautiful expression of you, with no right or wrong answers. Take the time to appreciate the vibrant expressions of your individuality.

From your heart center, begin to emit a soft, warm glow of white light. Slowly fill your aura with this loving, peaceful light. Allow it to grow brighter, burning away any remaining debris and healing any scars or rips in your aura. Slowly fill your field with the intention of love. Think your most beautiful, loving thoughts, and allow bliss to cascade over you. Colors begin to flow again into your aura, in a relaxed, tranquil manner. What colors do you see now? How do you feel physically and emotionally? Are you receiving any information or message? Relax in this state for a few moments longer, feeling the joy and acceptance from your heart.

Take a slow, deep breath and begin to come back to your physical body and the present moment. Take your time as you ease back into physical awareness. Open your eyes and again embrace yourself in grace and love. Stretch your muscles, wiggle your toes, and adjust your body as needed. You've done a great job and can be happy with all you are learning about your subtle energy system.

Please take time now with your HeartGlow journal to write about your Aura Wash experience and any reflections you may have. This exercise should be done at least once a week—especially after you've been in large crowds of people, such as in a hospital or a shopping mall. When you keep your aura clear and bright, you're free to radiate your unique light!

If you are cleansing the auric field of a family member or friend, follow the same process except now you are focusing on their field instead of your own in your mind's eye. It's best to ask permission before working with someone else's energy, so do follow proper energy etiquette by checking in with them first. This can be done directly through conversation or on the soul level with your HeartGlow dialogue. Journal your reflections for each person you are working with separately in your notebook. Be sure to note any changes you perceive in health, behavior, and attitude in the days following the Aura Wash exercise.

EXERCISE 4: GET YOUR GLOW ON:
LIGHT UP YOUR ENERGY CENTERS

Now we'll begin exploring the body's energy centers, also known as chakras. The only way to truly appreciate these centers is to discover them on your own. I'll borrow from our earlier metaphor of gems and jewels to guide you through this exercise. This is an in-depth method and can take an hour or more to do, so please set aside enough time and privacy for your exploration.

Start with the HeartGlow Primer to get into the proper mindset for this work. By setting the mood and intention, we accomplish more.

When you're sitting in a relaxed, focused state, put your attention on the center of your palms. Continue to breathe slowly and deeply through your nose, but also feel your breath in your hands. Start to feel your energy pulsing from your palm centers. Begin to imagine beautiful crystals glimmering at the center of each palm. Allow your light to glisten through these gems of your palm centers. How do your hands feel? Can you sense the energy surging through them? How large are your crystals? What do they look like?

Continue this exercise with the seven major energy centers in your body. Picture a vibrant jewel at each point on your body where the energy center lives. Allow your creative process to show you which gems reside in you. As you get to each center, light it up, allowing your inner glow to illuminate each crystal. What colors are your jewels? Do they follow a determined shade or have a unique hue? No matter what, it's good.

Take a deep breath and focus your attention on each major center individually, beginning at your first center at the base of your spine and working up your body to the seventh center, at the top of your head. Light each energy center with the spectrum of colors, and then repeat for each center. For example, bring your attention to your first center, allow it to glow a beautiful white light, then transfer the color to red, then orange, yellow, green, blue, indigo, and violet. Repeat this rainbow light show for each major center. Notice how each center feels and behaves. How does your body feel? Are you receiving any intuitive signals? Does any one center feel stronger or weaker to you?

After you work your way up your body's major centers, take a deep breath and ask Spirit with loving intention if there is anything you need to know or do for yourself, your child, or someone else. Be open to anything you may receive, keeping in mind it could come as a picture, a word, a feeling, or a whisper.

After a few moments of stillness, gently allow yourself to come back to the present moment. As always, write your experiences and reflections in your HeartGlow journal. This exercise should be done at least once a month—more often if you're dealing with significant imbalances. You can go back and revisit each center individually in another exercise if you discover areas to work on. This new energy-center knowledge will be built upon in future parent and child exercises, so be sure you construct a solid personal foundation.

SUMMARY OF KEY POINTS

HeartGlow is living with an intuitive heart. It is the conscious awareness of Divine energy radiating from our core. By opening your mind to the possibilities, you will be able to develop skills and heighten your sensitivities. You will make use of your loving connections to enhance communication, utilize energy healing, and restore balance in daily living.

Energy is our great power within. The human energy system has three primary subsystems: an energy field, energy centers, and energy pathways. The human energy field, also known as the aura or biofield, encompasses all living things and provides clues to those using their heightened sense of perception on the health and overall well-being of a person or thing.

The dogma of fixed belief is by far more cumbersome to carry than the light in your own heart. Divine guidance comes to us openly and freely, but we must use energy expertise to decipher the message.

Most people relate to the concept of channeling through its softer term *intuition*. The processes of clairvoyance, clairaudience, and clairsentience play a key role in understanding the nature of HeartGlow and how intuitive guidance works in your body and personal energy field. Science and spirituality meet as we begin to understand the amazing interactive talents of our hearts, minds, and bodies. Regardless of your chosen religion or spiritual path, take comfort in knowing that when we are at one with God, we are all one.

HeartGlow Hints for Intuitive Parenting

- Play with your intuition. How does your higher self talk to you?
- Avoid firm judgments and boundaries. There are no limits to the possibilities in every aspect of your life.
- Set an intention to be open to spiritual guidance.
- Get to know yourself through sensing your individual energy signature. How do you radiate?
- Light up your gems, or chakra centers, every morning for a clear start to your day.

3

The Field of
Intuitive Harmony

There is an unspoken language.
It comes from the silence and can't be heard by the ears,
only by the heart.

BABA HARI DASS, *ASHTANGA YOGA PRIMER*

Energy communication can be characterized as the transmission of images, thoughts, emotions, and sensations between our hearts and minds without additional means of communication. Although challenging to prove scientifically, it has been practiced in numerous cultures throughout the world, including the Aboriginal tribes of Australia, Native Americans, and other indigenous civilizations. Modern society has scores of anecdotal stories detailing energy communication, such as telepathy between twins, messages from animals, and a parent knowing of a loved one's injury hundreds of miles away. This field of study is in its infancy and poses exciting possibilities in communication enhancement between souls living together on this planet.

This is an opportunity for parents, caretakers, and medical practitioners to expand their knowledge of this unexplored horizon and raise their awareness of the intrinsic power within our energy fields. Together we can create a world in which this natural ability is nurtured, developed, and celebrated. It is time to raise our consciousness—not only for personal growth and development, but also to take steps in forming a new paradigm of intuitive parenting. My own experience sheds light on the intuitive heart's role in this fascinating phenomenon and its potential to positively affect your family.

A MESSAGE THROUGH THE SILENCE

Sleep wasn't coming easily one night. Getting appropriate rest on a firm bench in a hospital room was always a challenge. The room was sterile and cool with bright light and noise filtering in from the nurse's station just outside our door. Raegan lay motionless a few feet away, connected to an array of monitors and machines. We had been there for weeks, recovering from surgery to place a gastric feeding tube. She was now almost three years old and, for the most part, had been doing well. Although her initial prognosis and life expectancy were quite grim, this beautiful, angelic child had been thriving, despite her many physical and developmental limitations. Even though her disability was severe, we had settled into a comfortable groove—until now.

The feeding tube had been placed for hydration and to bolster nutrition, as she was increasingly having trouble swallowing liquids without choking. She took hours to bottle feed, sputtering and gasping loudly, conveying what a challenge it was to manage the task. Even though liquids were a struggle, Raegan could eat pureed foods like a champ—mashed potatoes, yogurt, and virtually any baby food. She enjoyed every bite, and we adored sharing meal times with her. Now those blissful memories seemed distant as her body lay lifeless and her eyes closed, with only the sounds of the equipment penetrating the air.

In this bleak moment, it seemed that everything that could go wrong did go wrong. The complications following the procedure were significant: a twisted stomach, inaccurate medications, and uncontrollable seizures. Each issue seemed to be addressed as it arose, yet Raegan wasn't doing well and we didn't know why. Her brilliant smile and joyful laugh had been absent for days now. The doctors just kept repeating that special-needs children are at greater risk for complications when undergoing medical procedures and she would take longer to recover from the swelling.

Things just didn't seem right to me. I understood what I was being told by the medical team, yet I just kept feeling as if something was being missed. My pleas for more tests were met with condescending remarks about over-reactive parents, and I was advised not to question the wisdom and experience of a gifted surgeon. As my daughter lay dying, I said a prayer of surrender to God: "Dear Lord, you know best ... please take care of my girl. Ease her pain. Whatever you want, just please show me the way to help her." Head drooping and shoulders hunched in resignation, I sighed deeply and continued to quietly weep.

Sitting there in the dark, physically and emotionally exhausted, warm tears rolling down my face, the phrase *it's growing* popped into my mind. Startled awake from my vacant gaze at the floor, I asked aloud, "What's growing?" Her reply was immediate, *"In my throat, Mommy."* I leaped from my position on the bench to my daughter's side and said to her in a gentle voice, "Are you trying to tell me something, AngelBaby?" A resounding *Yes* flooded my body. She remained sleeping with no physical indication that she was communicating with me. This time I knew it wasn't an angel or spirit guide trying to get my attention; Raegan herself was reaching out to me for help. I didn't know how she was doing it, but I believed with all my heart it was truth she was conveying. In the morning, I would press for immediate medical intervention to see what *it's growing* actually meant.

The surgical team was resistant to listening to anything I said. When I explained my concerns came directly from my daughter, they literally rolled their eyes. It was obvious the surgeons judged me to be overemotional, a bit flaky, and inexperienced in medical matters. I agree at the time I was not a picture of professionalism—worn jeans, T-shirt, and an aqua-aura crystal hanging around my neck, not to mention needing a long hot shower and a good night's sleep. They seemed to disapprove of my New Age nature and kept suggesting I go home and "take something to relax." I *knew* I was not to leave her side. A number of the staff nurses, however, showed support and said, "Mom usually knows best."

After weeks of posturing, while our daughter got worse by the day, the doctors finally ordered a barium swallow study to evaluate her digestive tract. In the simplest terms, Raegan was correct. A surgical stitch had been misplaced during her procedure, causing scar tissue to rapidly grow around it, blocking her esophagus and leaving her unable to swallow. Now it was apparent that this grave circumstance was not due to her disability or preexisting condition. She was a victim of a surgical mistake and was calling out for help.

"We haven't seen anything like this in twenty-five years," said the lead surgeon. "We're still not exactly sure how it occurred." Beads of sweat surfaced on his bald head as he quickly went on, "Unfortunately . . . it will be unlikely she'll be able to eat by mouth again, but at least she has the G-tube for her nutrition. I don't think it will affect her quality of life much, as limited as she already is. Anything I can do for you?" he asked a bit timidly.

My face growing hot, I tried to contain my anger and stammered, "Yes, listen to me next time. Please listen to the moms." Turning away from him, tears flowed heavily as I realized the months of growing scar tissue meant Raegan would not again enjoy her favorite squash or sweet vanilla pudding. One of the few pleasures in her fragile life was being taken away with the slip of a stitch. The doctors viewed her as being already profoundly flawed, so why would this matter at all? It was infuriating.

Raegan was required to have additional surgery to correct the problem. In fact, she had numerous procedures trying to reverse the harm done. Our confidence shaken in the original surgical team, we transferred hospitals and began the task of recovery. Throughout the many months she was hospitalized, Raegan continued to teach me how to use our hearts to talk. This unusual form of communication seemed especially acute during times of crisis and when we were both sleeping. At that point, I decided I would no longer make any decision regarding her care without checking in via our heart connection. It seemed to me Raegan was operating from a higher place.

THE ENERGY OF THE HEART

Where exactly is that place? This unique experience with my daughter led me to dive headfirst into an unknown sea. I began seeking out other intuitive families, furthering my education, exploring scientific research and case studies on metaphysics, theology, psychic ability, and energy medicine. Although I always believed in the power of intuition, here was an ideal opportunity to use the ability for something truly remarkable, enhancing communication for families in need.

Unlike documented telepathic experiments, our experience was not an intellectual pursuit or academic exercise. There were no sci-fi enthusiasts sitting opposite one another trying to send triangles or wavy lines and then frantically tracking their results. Raegan's mental abilities were poor, yet she was able to get her message delivered and save her own life by using energy to communicate. This hails an opportunity for everyone, even those who have perceived physical or intellectual limitations, to greater express themselves in a new energetic way and improve their quality of life. Like Raegan, a child reaching out would be heard by those listening with their heart.

Rupert Sheldrake, biologist and author, is a leading researcher in subjects such as the nature of the mind, morphogenetic fields, and unexplained powers in animals. Sheldrake reports, "Morphic fields of social groups connect together members of the group even when they are many miles apart, and provide channels of communication through which organisms can stay in touch at a distance."[1] These energy fields, which surround all living things and extend far beyond our brains, provide an explanation for telepathy, animal communication, and other forms of channeling. The scientific work of Sheldrake demonstrates that energy communication is a natural experience between people, especially those who are familiar with one another and utilize skills of intention to expand the ability of their minds.

In one of Sheldrake's studies of telepathy between babies and nursing mothers, it was revealed that emotional closeness is a key factor in being better able to communicate telepathically. Since newborn babies are unable to speak, this shows a clear correlation in the telepathic possibilities inherent in traditional children, as well as those who have communication challenges throughout their lives.

HeartMath research director Rollin McCraty and his team have determined the heart generates a powerful field of electromagnetic energy. It is the largest field in our body and can be perceived by sophisticated instruments up to several feet away. Their research shows the heart's field clearly transforms as different emotions are felt. Most compelling, their evidence also indicates "energetic interactions involving the heart may underlie intuition and important aspects of human consciousness."[2] Scientific research is beginning to explain the complex energetic system of communication, which is occurring at all times within us. Taking this knowledge to heart and expanding our awareness, we can reveal a new language of energy, which can instruct, enhance, and transform the way we communicate with one another.

INTUITIVE HARMONY

Nobody has ever measured, not even poets,
how much a heart can hold.
—ZELDA FITZGERALD

The research and theories by Sheldrake, McCraty, and others clearly explain the science behind my personal experience with heart communication. This inspired me to begin teaching how we can take advantage of our natural connections to improve our lives. The simple facts being: our energy fields are able to exchange information in an accurate, appropriate, and timely manner; our loving connections to one another enhance the probability. Raegan saved her own life by telling me what was wrong, and she did it by using the intuitive heart of her subtle energy system. My own innate energy sensitivity allowed me to hear her.

As discussed in the last chapter, we all have a subtle energy system comprised of energy fields, energy centers, and energy pathways. In the HeartGlow program, we also explore the connections between the systems of individuals, particularly in parent-child relationships. A fundamental premise of my work is the existence of shared or common energy fields and being able to improve energy communication with positive actions and intentions.

The sacred bond between loved ones creates a common energy field, which I have named the Field of Intuitive Harmony. This is the place where our hearts meet. When we are in resonance within this field, energy communication and healing are possible. We have defined HeartGlow as a state of being, living with an intuitive heart. Thus, the goal of HeartGlow is to create, increase, and support resonance within our shared field, as well as to heighten sensitivities, to enhance energy communication and healing. The following diagram shows how the interconnected energy fields of a parent and child create the Field of Intuitive Harmony.

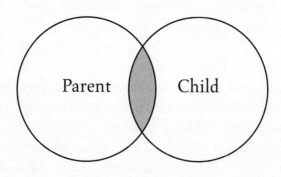

Now what do we mean by *resonance*? In his compelling work, *The Divine Matrix*, Gregg Braden describes resonance as "a fine-tuning of the subtle energy that brings us into balance with our world."[3] This harmony and balance is known to us through feelings of comfort when we are in our own homes or enjoying the company of our close friends. Think of it as being tuned in to and affected by the same energetic frequency, vibration, or wavelength. Actually, people instinctively understand the concept in relation to communication and relationships, often remarking about being in tune, on the same wavelength, or sharing a vibe with one another. Resonance is employed in a variety of disciplines, yet it has roughly the same meaning. Consider the following examples:

Resonance in Music. Several strings tuned to pitches that are harmonically related will vibrate even if only one of the strings is strummed. Thus, if a note is struck on a piano, the strings tuned to pitches that belong to the harmonic series of that note will also vibrate.

Resonance in Physics. In science, resonance is the process in which oscillations in a system are produced, maintained, or enhanced by means of a periodic transfer of energy from another oscillating system, whose frequency is identical to that of the first.

Resonance in Spirit. Resonance is recognized in spiritual practices, as shown with the principle of namasté: the God Light in me honors the God Light in you; when you are in that place in you, and I am in that place in me, we are One.

Resonance is an important component in HeartGlow, as it must exist before energy communication can be perceived. In the Field of Intuitive Harmony, our shared energy field, the potential for communication always exists. There is a constant flow of energy and information present; however, it is not often brought to our conscious awareness because we are not in resonance with one another. If our vibrations do not match, we do not perceive one another's information, even though it is already there waiting to be discovered. When we are tuned to the same frequency, when we are in harmony with one another, energy communication can be perceived. Our awareness and sensitivity to our family's individual and collective energies are powerful instruments in affecting positive change and opening the doors to energy communication. Skillfully playing our instruments in brilliant harmony, we can appreciate and savor the eloquent symphony of our lives.

I am often asked how parent-child heart communication differs from traditional telepathic or psychic messages. Love makes all the difference. Parents are able to access this energetic information due to the loving bonds they share with their children. Psychic messages, in my experience, often come from a clear detachment to the subject at hand, as opposed to the intimacy we are exploring here. Energy professionals have finely tuned sensitivities that enable entry to an array of vibrational realms. In my numerous years as a practitioner, I have witnessed astounding demonstrations of energetic precision from people throughout the world. Each specialist is unique in their methods and talents, which makes it all the more interesting to observe and garner knowledge.

In addition to emotional connectedness, DNA may also play a compelling role in energy communication. Can it be our genetic connection to our children gives us an added advantage in communication? Additional research on photons, energy fields, and cell communication just may support the theory of "once connected, always connected". Intuitively, I believe this to be so and look forward to science catching up with these exciting ideas. I find this especially gripping when pondering the relationship between a pregnant mother and her developing child. It is incredible to think of the energetic bonds being formed at this crucial time. Picture the Field of Intuitive Harmony delicately coming into being as we develop and grow within the womb. Expecting parents, honor the intimacy of your bonds by energetically reaching out to your developing child. It is never too early to send the intentions of love, comfort, and security.

Fortunately, HeartGlow is not limited to only biological relationships. I have quite a few clients who are adoptive parents and are able to utilize their loving bonds alone to communicate energetically. My stepson, Graham, is a great example of this. He and I have no biological tie whatsoever, yet at various points during his teenage years I was able to get mind's eye pictures of his whereabouts and actions. These occurrences were not exactly convenient for him, especially if he was trying to push his limits, but they were extremely valuable to us in establishing healthy rules and boundaries for our family. Now that he is grown, we often joke about how I knew what he was up to, even if he was halfway across town. Fortunately, our connection works both ways, as his own intuition lets him know when he should call home to touch base with us. Go ahead and try sending a message without the use of a phone or computer—it's fun!

In the first three chapters of this book, we have covered the foundation of information you will now need to build upon. Having an understanding of this material will better prepare you for the techniques and exercises we will explore throughout the remainder of the text. *Our goal in HeartGlow is to create, increase, and support resonance within our shared field as well as to heighten sensitivities and to enhance energy communication and healing.* The next three chapters will delve into encouraging energetic resonance through practices of sound, touch, and love.

HeartGlow Exercises

Now that you have an understanding of resonance and the Field of Intuitive Harmony, these next two exercises will help you explore your family's unique energy connections. You'll be amazed at what you will learn about your family and yourself. Please read through the exercises now and then review them again before you do them. Keep it fun and you'll enjoy the entire HeartGlow development process.

Exercise 5: Creating an Intuitive Heart Chart

We are going to create an Intuitive Heart Chart. You will need your HeartGlow journal and, if you want to be vibrant, colored pencils, crayons, and even fun stickers. This exercise should be done first on your own and then again with your children, if you feel they would enjoy it.

First, begin by going to a blank page in your journal. On this page draw a large circle in the center. This circle represents you and your personal energy field, so choose an appropriate color. What color screams to you? I have always gravitated toward red, so I use red for this particular exercise. Now select a color for your child and draw another circle interconnecting with yours. You should have two linking circles. Use a different color for each of your children and add their circles to your page so that each intersects your circle. For example, if you are a mother of three children, your page would look something like this:

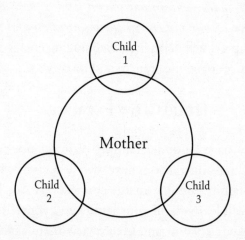

Remember, the areas that overlap represent our Field of Intuitive Harmony—the place our hearts meet. See how large each field is and how small the overlap is in comparison? Our souls are individual vibrant lights, which do interconnect, yet do not consume one another. As important as our connections are, we must realize that each person, parent, or child has her own path, his own journey to travel in this lifetime. On our amazing, magical tour of life, we have chosen one another to be partners—to learn from, laugh with, and grow together.

Looking at your family members individually, creatively write your intentions for the relationship in the remaining space on the page. Use your crayons, stickers, or drawings to express your heart's desire for the connection with your child. Love, peace, trust, or communication? What do you intend? Do you have specific issues you wish to address, such as talking to each other daily or playing together more? Start at the surface, then dig deeper. We are not writing projections of who we think the other should be or what he should do. We are also not demanding material possessions. If possessions come to your mind, look further to what they may represent. Security? Acceptance?

Express your intentions on the page, realizing the artistry of the process will help open you to higher dimensions and help you access wishes even you may not consciously know you have. Complete this process for each of your children. Take your time and enjoy yourself. You may encounter some emotional rough spots, so realize these are gifts as well and can lead you to a greater understanding of yourself and your child. Fill your page with your imaginative illustrations.

After you are done with the Intuitive Heart Chart, I would like you to actively contemplate this exercise and your intentions for your relationships energetically. Find a comfortable place in your home; begin with the HeartGlow Primer to get yourself in a relaxed yet alert state. Take a deep breath and exhale slowly. Visualize your Intuitive Heart Chart. See the intentions you have set afloat in your mind and energy field. Allow the words to turn into pictures or even songs. Comprehend all of what you are asking of yourself and the Universe. Ask Spirit: what actions do I take to realize my intentions? Allow the answers to flow into you.

Within the stillness, listen for the whispers of wisdom, which come from your highest self. Be patient and know guidance will be coming, if it is not readily apparent.

Now picture your child laughing and smiling. Visualize their face ... their form ... their energy. Add yourself to the picture and see the two of you laughing together, holding hands and playing. What does your combined energy feel like? Can you feel the resonance? Let go of any doubts or fears of past actions or behaviors in your relationship. Replace any negative image or emotion with love and understanding. This is the place of acceptance. This is the place of kindness and unity. You are in the Field of Intuitive Harmony. In this sacred space, tell your child all you wish for the relationship. Share your visions and dreams. Take the time to hear what your child may have to say to you in return. If words escape you, send pictures or symbols, like a heart or maybe a bouquet of flowers. Take as much time as you need in this special place. When you feel your visit is complete, say goodbye with loving actions and words. Embrace your child; kiss each child softly on the forehead. Always know you can journey here again, as often as you wish.

When you come back to the present moment, take time to write your reflections in your HeartGlow journal. If you received any messages from your child or from Spirit, please write them down to reflect upon. You may modify your Intuitive Heart Chart as often as you wish. Also remember to energetically travel to your Field of Intuitive Harmony to set the intentions there as well. When you begin to recognize the unique resonance of your parent-child connection, you can access it by simply opening your heart and entering.

If you choose to do this exercise with your children, bring it to their level and really have fun with it. Make sure they are the center circle in their own Intuitive Heart Chart and teach them how to make interlocking circles for each of their parents and siblings. How do they see each of these relationships and what do they wish for them? You just may be surprised by the moving and significant insights children have. Reflect upon what your children's charts reveal about your connection.

EXERCISE 6: DREAM EXPLORATION

Dreams are a powerful way in which information is energetically conveyed to us. Whether images are archetypal, prophetic, or literal, the signs and symbols can lead us to greater truth and understanding of our personal circumstances. Often, we are more open in our dream state—our egos and personalities are at rest, leaving room for enhanced receptivity. You can not only receive insight from higher sources but also poignant messages from those you love.

Often there were times during Raegan's hospitalizations when I would be woken from a sound sleep with a sharp image burning in my mind. In one specific instance, an intense bright color green flashed before me. As medical professionals may recognize, this is the exact color of bile from our digestive system. Believing this was a warning, I got up from bed to check on Raegan and discovered bile backing up into her stomach and out her drainage tube. Here was another complication from surgery: an adhesion had formed in her intestines and the flow had been blocked, requiring yet another procedure to correct. An energy message was again alerting me to an actual physical problem in her body.

I hope you find these specific examples of Raegan's success in communicating with me encouraging for your own pursuits. Although I am now quite savvy about Raegan's particular medical issues, at the time I had no knowledge of bile's color or function in the body. Being nonverbal, she used the form of communication which came naturally to her—the energy of her heart. We can all do the same by opening our hearts, transmuting limited perceptions, and embracing a world of pure potentiality. Just imagine what your child can tell you!

Allie, one of my HeartGlow moms, has been very encouraged by the clairvoyant messages she receives in regard to the care of her children. Often posing a question to the Universe before going to bed at night, she then records the mind's eye pictures that float back to her in response. Concerned her teenage daughter was becoming quiet and distant, she asked what she could do to assist with the situation. A large red stop sign was the image sent back. "Stop? Just stop?" she asked. Allie took this as a message to back off from pestering her daughter with questions and to basically give her some space. Within a few days, her quiet teen's mood shifted and she thanked her mom for the breathing room. "I'm just glad you stopped. You were really starting to bug me, Mom," said the girl as she bounded out of the house to see her friends. Smiling to herself, Allie was happy she trusted the intuitive message she received.

In this exercise, I would like you to begin exploring your own channels of energy communication by setting intentions before sleep and recording your dreams. You can choose to use your HeartGlow journal or select a specific dream journal to write your notes. Some people find it useful to have a microcassette or digital recorder by the bed to speak their dream messages, instead of trying to write before having coffee in the morning. Find a method which is most comfortable for you. I do advise making your notes *before* you leave your bed in the morning. Details are quickly forgotten once our feet touch the floor. This exercise is to be started just prior to going to sleep and finished upon waking.

Let's begin again with the HeartGlow Primer. Put yourself into a relaxed state by sitting comfortably on the edge of your bed with your back straight. Take a few deep breaths, inhaling slowly through your nose and exhaling slowly out your mouth. Allow the frustrations of the day to leave you, floating far out of your mind. Simply relax. Shake loose any body part you feel tension clinging to. Reach up and run your hands through your hair a few times, slightly tugging your hair, as you run your nails across your scalp. Embrace yourself by wrapping your arms snuggly around your body; send yourself love, acceptance, and understanding. Move your hands and arms to a comfortable position on your lap. Slowly, take another deep breath. Say aloud or to yourself, "I am Light. I am Peace. I am Love."

With a clear heart and mind, state your intentions and pose any questions to the Universe. Family, health, career path? This is all about your discovery. What is it that you want to know? Ask for clarity and guidance on the topic you desire to explore further, such as, "Spirit, I am open to your guidance and information. Make clear any actions that would be helpful to my family at this time." Find your own words for this sacred conversation. After stating your business in your heart, mind, and journal, you can settle down for a night's sleep. Take it slow and start with only one issue. Pose this same question every night for a week. If you send a chaotic message, you just may get a chaotic response.

When you wake in the morning, jot down any notes from your dreams in writing or voice recording. Don't force the issue and only speak what you can easily recall. At this point, you are only making a notation and will go back to the information at another time to evaluate. After making your notes, simply go on about your day. If other information comes to you throughout the day, write it down and later transfer it to your journal.

When you have the time and space to examine your dream journal, take a look at what you have written and elaborate on any ideas or concepts that seem clearer to you now. When you look at different components of your dreams, ask yourself these questions:

1. How did the dream make me feel emotionally?

2. Does a person, item, or thing in my dream represent anything specific to me?

3. Do I recall any particular colors, numbers, or names?

4. Do I recognize anyone's energy signature?

5. Is there a message related to my specific intentions or questions?

Spend some quality time contemplating your dream. Record each reflection in your journal and then . . . release it. There is no need to hold on to any one thing. You've taken it in, processed it consciously, and now you can let it go. This is the beginning of your dream dialogue—or your *awareness* of the dialogue. Be mindful. What is energy based, and what may be the ego's fearful rambling? Raegan's messages were simple and to the point, without attachment or judgment. It is what it is. Try to remember that if it comes from fear, it is the ego talking and not the higher energies of yourself or someone else. It takes time to tell the difference, but it becomes easier as you begin to live with an intuitive heart.

Examine your dreams whenever you feel called to do so. If it starts to feel too burdensome, stop and begin again when you find joy in the process. Make it a family affair by asking your children about their dreams over breakfast. It is fun to discover that family members often have similar dreams, which is a shining example of our Field of Intuitive Harmony in action.

SUMMARY OF KEY POINTS

Energy communication can be characterized as the transmission of images, thoughts, emotions, and sensations between our hearts and minds without additional means of communication. It has been practiced in diverse cultures throughout the world, including the Aboriginal tribes of Australia, Native Americans, and other indigenous civilizations.

There are scores of anecdotes detailing energy communication in modern society, such as telepathy between twins, messages from animals, and a parent knowing of a loved one's injury hundreds of miles away. Together we can create a world in which this natural ability is nurtured, developed, and celebrated. It is time to raise our consciousness—not only for personal growth and development, but also to take steps in forming a new paradigm of intuitive parenting. This presents an opportunity for everyone, even those who have perceived physical or intellectual limitations, to greater express themselves in a new energetic way and improve their quality of life.

The scientific work of Rupert Sheldrake clearly demonstrates energy communication is a natural experience between people, especially those who are familiar with one another and utilize skills of intention to expand the ability of their minds. Emotional closeness is a key factor in being more able to communicate telepathically. Rollin McCraty and his team have determined the heart generates a powerful field of electromagnetic energy. Scientific research is beginning to explain the complex energetic system of communication occurring at all times within us. This research shows the heart's field clearly transforms as different emotions are felt. Taking this knowledge to heart and expanding our awareness, we can reveal a new language of energy, which can instruct, enhance, and transform the way we communicate with one another.

Our energy fields are able to exchange information in an accurate, appropriate, and timely manner. Our loving connections to one another enhance the probability. The sacred bond between loved ones creates a common energy field, which I have named the Field of Intuitive Harmony. This is the place where our hearts meet. When we are in resonance within this field, energy communication and healing is possible. Resonance is defined as the harmony and balance known to us through feelings of comfort when in our own homes or enjoying the company of our close friends. Think of it as being tuned in to and affected by the same energetic frequency, vibration, or wavelength. If our vibrations do not match, we do not perceive one another's information, even though it is already there, waiting to be discovered.

The goal of HeartGlow is to create, increase, and support resonance within our shared field as well as to heighten sensitivities and to enhance energy communication and healing. When we are tuned in to the same frequency, when we are in harmony with one another, energy communication can be perceived. Our awareness and sensitivity to our family's individual and collective energies are powerful instruments in affecting positive change and opening the doors to energy communication. Parents are able to access this energetic information due to the loving bonds they share with their children.

HEARTGLOW HINTS FOR INTUITIVE PARENTING

- Your connection with your child is like no other in the Universe. Take the time to discover its wonder and unique resonance.
- Our greatest pain can often lead us to our deepest truth. Be patient and allow the healing power of time and reflection to serve you.
- Closing your eyes just may expand your vision. Give yourself the gift of looking within for the answers to life's questions.

- Take a look at your day-to-day behavior. How do you waste your energy? Gossip? Worry? Seeking drama? Make a different choice and reap the rewards.
- Visualize a rainbow bridge connecting your heart to the ones you love.

PART II

Raising the Vibration: HeartGlow Techniques

4

The Resonance of Sound

A bird does not sing because it has an answer.
It sings because it has a song.

CHINESE PROVERB

Sound therapy is a broad term used to describe a healing modality in which sound or vibration addresses health deficiencies in people. These conditions can be physical, emotional, mental, or spiritual in nature and affect those in all walks of life. Originally developed from the work of Dr. Alfred Tomatis, sound therapy has been explored for over fifty years with new discoveries just beginning to be associated with the well-being and balance of our subtle energy systems.

In understanding sound as an energetic modality, we must correlate this creative healing art as an expression of Divine energy. Religious and spiritual healing through music has been known throughout the ages and cultures worldwide. Shamans and tribal elders have used drums to represent the heartbeat of Mother Earth in attuning the ailing with Divine healing energy. In our modern society, it is common when enjoying a talented vocalist or musician to refer to them as having a gift from God. The vibration of the Universe is recognized intuitively in their song as it resonates in our hearts, triggering us to remember our connectedness to the All.

MUSIC OF THE HEART

*Music expresses that which cannot be put into words
and that which cannot remain silent.*
—VICTOR HUGO, FRENCH DRAMATIST, NOVELIST,
AND POET (1802–1885)

Looking out the window of our new hospital room, I breathed deeply, trying to muster up enthusiasm for our new circumstances. Unpacking a small bag into an even smaller drawer, I watched the snow lightly dance in the narrow airspace between the buildings. We had arrived at Children's Hospital Boston late the night before via ambulance to begin a recovery regimen with a new team of doctors. Now here we were, hours from home and feeling more alone than ever before.

Mark stayed behind for work, so Raegan and I would need to cope with only phone calls and weekend visits from Daddy. This place was huge—and a bit intimidating. We were high up on the eighth floor in a surgical ward bustling with noise and activity. Fear crept into my mind as I worried I had made the wrong decision to leave Maine. We had not yet met our new doctor and, arriving so late at night, I didn't have the chance to get my bearings. "Please God, give me a sign I have made the right decision," I whispered.

The door opened suddenly and a vibrant young woman came in. "Good morning and welcome, Miss Raegan," she said in a cheerful tone. "I'm here to make sure you are settling in. How are you doing, Mom? Would you like to walk around a bit and grab a cup of coffee while I get to know Raegan?" she asked sweetly. A smile spread across my face as I watched her approach Raegan and begin to talk about her stuffed animals and the cartoons on TV. Raegan's eyes widened in fascination as she listened to the delightful woman talk. I knew she was in good hands for the few moments it would take me to find some caffeine.

Still watching them over my shoulder, I walked out of the room and abruptly collided with a man in the hall. "Oh, my goodness. I am so sorry," I sputtered in embarrassment.

"No need to apologize. Please excuse me," he said, softly touching my arm to make sure I was steady on my feet. He was an older gentleman, with the kindest eyes, immaculately dressed in a suit and tie. A bit startled, I watched him walk into the room next to ours and say good morning to the folks inside. My heart still pounding, I realized I had just about knocked down the world-famous Dr. T. Berry Brazelton.

Like many parents, I had been familiar with Dr. Brazelton's achievements in child development through his books and seeing his smiling face over the years on countless television programs. Now, here he was, in person, caring for families directly. Although Dr. Brazelton would not be involved in Raegan's care, I knew his presence was God giving me the sign I had asked for. Of all the doctors I could have plowed into and never recognized, *he* was put in my path. A chance encounter in the hall showed me we were in the company of some of the best specialists in the world; Raegan would be well cared for.

The signs continued to come to me as I walked around the hospital, taking in the atmosphere. Everything seemed to be glowing. Giant fish tanks, animated displays, and colorful artwork decorated the lobby. People of every background milled about, purchasing balloons for their children or getting a quick bite to eat from the coffee shop. The energy was busy, yet clearly positive. Finding a cinnamon scone and latte, I made my way back to the room with a near bounce in my step. It was obvious now; we had come to a place of great healing.

Late in the afternoon, our first roommates arrived—a young child just out of surgery and his mother. The nurse told me the family was from Jordan in the Middle East and could not speak English. We would need to do our best in sharing the bathroom and amenities with limited communication. The mother was covered from head to toe in a dark dress and burka, making it difficult to see her eyes or the facial expressions we so often rely on when speaking is not possible. She hovered cautiously near her child as he tossed and turned, obviously still groggy from the procedure. I would flash an encouraging smile every time I walked by but was unsure if my intention was getting through. Spending most of the afternoon on the phone with our respective families, we didn't have much opportunity to speak or reach out to one another.

As the day grew long, the activity on the floor quieted and it was time to prepare ourselves and our children for bed. The room was hushed and the lights dim, trying to ease our little patients into slumber. While in the hospital, I had taken the habit of sleeping in sweatpants, a T-shirt, and a cardigan sweater so I would still be somewhat dressed if problems arose in the night, as they often did. It had been months since I had taken the time and energy to wear makeup or do any real self-care. Looking in the mirror after brushing my teeth, I knew I was long overdue for a haircut, a nap, and a little time for me. Blinking away tears, I sprawled alongside Raegan in her bed and began to talk softly to her about her kitties at home and more pleasant times to come.

The Jordanian mother rushed by our bed toward the bathroom to change for the night. When she reemerged several moments later, I could hardly believe my eyes. There before me was one of the most beautiful women I had ever seen—long, dark hair cascading down her shoulders, captivating eyes, and a brilliant smile. She wore jewel-tone pajamas of purple satin and exuded pure grace. Stopping at the foot of the bed, she smiled and reached out for Raegan. "Beautiful," she said, massaging my daughter's feet tenderly. I smiled in appreciation as we connected for the first time, mom to mom and heart to heart. We both knew our shared room was a place of comfort and healing for our little ones.

As I lay with my daughter, softly singing her to sleep, I could hear this mother tenderly singing to her son in Arabic. Two mothers, in some ways worlds apart, could not be more similar as their heart songs lofted to the heavens. There we were, together, comforting our children through song and the energy of our love. Closing my eyes, my heart soared as I could sense the energy of each parent and child in the hospital, each parent and child in the country, then every parent and child in the world. Visualizing beams of love light all over the globe, we were illuminating the Universe. At that moment, resonance intensified, I realized my connection to everyone and everything, each of us beautiful notes in the amazing song of life.

HEALING SOUNDS

There are significant advantages to employing sound as a healing modality for our children. In addition to the documented medical benefits of hearing and speech improvement, there is also significant basis for addressing learning delays and disabilities. In a 1995 study, sound-therapy specialists Elizabeth and Derek Rintel reported "gains in tests of Auditory Discrimination, Reading Ability, Reading Comprehension and Spelling" after exposure to sound therapy for a period of sixteen weeks. The research specifically examined classrooms implementing Joudry Sound Therapy Tapes, which are recordings of high-frequency filtered classical music.[1]

According to Jonathan Goldman, a leader in the study of sound healing, a basic principle of this method of healing is the belief in resonance. As stated in the previous chapter, resonance is being tuned in to and affected by the same energetic frequency, vibration, or wavelength. All things in the Universe, including the Universe itself, have a certain vibration and thus a sound. Sound healing presumes that by balancing and harmonizing the vibrations within our physical and auric bodies, healing will naturally occur.[2] This premise leads to a discussion on sound as not only a musical expression but also as a powerful tool of vibration, tones, and frequencies.

Traditional sound methods primarily focus on auditory stimulation and audio-vocal exercises to correct hearing abnormalities or to promote stress reduction. Here we'll explore the holistic approaches of music and vibration, which heighten our sensitivities and increase resonance within the Field of Intuitive Harmony, escorting us into a new world of energy communication and healing.

MUSIC

One good thing about music,
when it hits you, you feel no pain.
—BOB MARLEY

According to the American Music Therapy Association, music therapy is a well-established healthcare profession that utilizes music to address emotional, social, physical, and cognitive needs of patients in all age groups. This medium is a noninvasive approach that is often compared with physical and occupational therapy as a viable healthcare service. Although not as widely used as the aforementioned, music therapy is growing in use and popularity in early intervention programs and for children enrolled in special education. Methods employed by the therapists include singing, instrument play, and a variety of musical activities, all designed to prompt change in areas thought to be nonmusical in nature, such as intellectual, behavioral, and academic growth.

While staying in the hospital in Boston, Raegan was visited a number of times by a music therapist. He walked through the halls playing a guitar and singing cheerful songs. Her face lit up as he strummed, her hand reaching toward him to feel the vibrations of the instrument. No matter which room he was in, people gravitated toward the sounds of the music, joy rising in their hearts as the energy intensified. I could see the beautiful colors of their auric fields dancing as they experienced a respite from their medical worries and fears.

The possibilities for our families inherent in music are astounding. Clinical research and practical application indicate that music therapy facilitates development in sensory, motor, cognitive, and communication skills. It is important to note that these modalities are not limited to the use and application by a certified medical practitioner. Music is being explored in homes and by complementary alternative practitioners to create balance not only in the physical body but also in the chakras and energy fields of clients. These healings can take the form of drumming, chanting, and listening to soft music for relaxation and stress reduction—simple yet valuable techniques which can be put into practice directly by parents and caretakers.

My friend and colleague Deirdre Drennen is an intuitive musician who uses the sound of her voice in addition to her lap harp to attune clients to higher levels of vibration. When I had my first healing with Deirdre, I was surprised by the actual tingling I felt in my body as my energy centers cleared. It was relaxing yet also uplifting. When Deirdre visits Raegan, she gets on the floor with her and sings her name over and over in different tunes and tones, "Raegan Aria, Raegan Aria." Seeing my daughter so captivated by this, my husband and I now also tone with Raegan on a regular basis. She will often join in, with exactly the proper pitch. Mark, who has been a performing tenor for years, affirms Raegan is his favorite singing partner.

One vital component of the work I do with families is strengthening energetic bonds between parents and their children. Life can weigh heavily with the anxieties of work, bills, health, and other day-to-day pressures. We often do not take the time to connect with our loved ones on a deep level, as it is tough enough merely providing for them. Parents frequently speak of the resentment and guilt they feel for the lack of connectedness to their children during times of stress. Music, I have found, can bridge the emotional and energetic gap. By applying a few simple practices, your family can be closer than ever before:

- Sing together. Whether to the radio, karaoke, or at church, singing will raise your vibration and openness to each other.
- Have a family music night once a week. Each week a member of the family picks a new CD to listen to together. Talk about why you like it, what memories are stirred, and how it makes you feel. You just may learn something about one another.
- Grab some instruments and jam! They can be professional or homemade. It only matters that you are making music together. Regardless of age, every family member can participate with a drum, tambourine, or even a rattle.
- Make a commitment to experience live music more often. Go to concerts, theater, and festivals. Can you see the auras of the performers as they play?
- Take a music class. Expand your knowledge of music and activate your creative genius through piano, vocal, or string lessons. Allow each member of the family to choose a musical activity that resonates with them.

VIBRATION

Vibrational sensitivity and empathy,
it seems, are fundamental human tendencies,
with roots going back to the womb.
—PENNEY PEIRCE, *FREQUENCY*

The field of vibration therapy is currently being explored by both traditional and alternative practitioners for its unique contribution to health and wellness. Although the perspectives differ significantly, both approaches offer valid directions in which to take your journey. A technique well known to both camps is vibration massage, often used for reducing stress, easing fatigued muscles, and releasing physical tension. However, the field of study has gone far beyond the personal healthcare benefits of a massaging chair or a heated vibrating footbath. The future of vibration therapy may be the key that unlocks the door to a new perspective on healing.

In traditional medical settings, recent vibration research has been closely associated with bone preservation. In a study by M. Tylee and colleagues, the use of a vibration platform in treating patients with spinal cord injuries is explored to determine its effect on maintaining bone density. Although the research indicates numerous avenues for future study, it was able to clearly demonstrate that the human body "can be represented as a linear mechanical system during vibration therapy."[3] This discovery is an essential stepping stone for future pioneers in vibration research aimed at discovering healing techniques appropriate for patients facing a variety of bone disorders and other illnesses, including osteoporosis, leukemia, and arthritis.

An alternative approach in vibration therapy is to use the frequencies of a tuning fork or crystal to balance the vibration in the auric field or physical body of a client. The approach is similar to other alternative modalities in the use of a massage table and being in a relaxed connected state, yet it then incorporates the use of a specific vibration tool to obtain the desired balance for the client. The tuning fork is played on the instrument of the human body, much like tuning a piano to the correct key. The practitioner restores the balance through the vibration of the tool.

In a therapeutic setting, vibration mats and toys are used in sessions with children to provide comfort and sensory stimulation. Children with hearing impairments are able to experience music through its unique vibration signature. There is significant practical feedback on these methodologies and a great variety of related care products on the market; however, clinical research is not yet comprehensive.

One compelling factor in vibration research is in the now quantifiable frequencies of energy healers. Author Walter Weston reports healers are measured to have brain wave frequencies of 7.83 hertz and can produce more than 200 volts of energy.[4] I find this information intriguing yet intuitively believe there are healers across a variety of the spectrums which we cannot measure, at least not yet. It is important we do not label or restrict those who do not fit into a preset paradigm or belief system.

Our Universe is creative and multifaceted. We are here to expand our perspectives, not to limit the possibilities. I have witnessed healers, medical doctors, and holistic practitioners do astonishing things. The important note is: the intuitive healing arts are now gaining scientific validity, which can only lead to additional advancements in study and practice. The amazing correlation yet to be made points to future vibration research expanding the measurement of and attunement to the exact frequency of Divine healing energy.

This possibility alone poses the most promise for children in our society. Allowing the allopathic and holistic models to be bridged by the acceptance of energetic healing will forever shift our world. Embracing heart-centered intuitive approaches in combination with the growing scientific knowledge of energy and its frequencies will expand the perspectives and raise the consciousness of practitioners and their clients. The world is beginning to comprehend the healing vibration of the Universe, which resonates within all people, places, and things.

Sensing the earth's natural vibrations can come easily to some, yet it takes additional work for others, including me. While completing my doctorate degree in metaphysics, I was also an energy apprentice to psychic Bill Sengel. An eccentric and well-read energy practitioner, Bill lives in the mountains of western Maine and provided me with immense tangible experience to back up the many theories and philosophies I was studying. Walking through the woods on his property, he would taunt and test me about sensing the earth's energies: "Which direction does it flow? What spot? How do you see it in your mind's eye?" He playfully shouted instructions as I trampled up and down the hills searching for a vortex to ride. This unconventional classroom provided me with the knowledge and enhanced perception I needed to appreciate the subtle energies of our Earth.

Incorporating vibration techniques at home can be done in a variety of ways; simply follow your intuition as to what might work for your family. Several clients whose children are considered by doctors to be on the autism spectrum report their kids as having a sensitivity and fondness for vibration in appliances, stones, and specific places on their property. I have found it best to let children take the lead and support what they are naturally drawn to. One child in particular collected rocks and felt comforted by them. It wasn't until the mother took a closer look that she realized each rock had bits of quartz embedded somewhere in them. Then it was easy to acknowledge that her child naturally gravitated toward these healing stones. I have seen similar traits in other children with regard to shells, leaves, shapes, and colors.

My client Don not only uses his HeartGlow skills with his children but also with his father, who has Alzheimer's disease. Watching his dad slowly deteriorate in awareness and communication abilities at a nursing facility has been painful for Don. Constantly striving to remain connected, he brings in items from home, realizing the energy of certain favorite things stir a reaction from his father and even stimulate conversation about their past. A beloved religious medallion seems to provide the most comfort and healing for them both. The Field of Intuitive Harmony is there for all to explore, regardless of whether you are the parent or the child. Don demonstrates this beautifully by tapping in to the vibrations and honoring the energetic connections with items he shared with his father.

Remember, everything has a vibration. Your resonance with an object, person, or thing may offer you a unique opportunity to tap in to Divine energy. Here are some suggestions on how you can experience good vibrations:

- Decorate yourself and your home with natural stones and crystals for their beauty and healing properties.
- Use a quartz crystal, tuning fork, or vibrating massager to activate your own or your family's energy centers.
- Play with rocks! As a family, collect and track your sensitivity to certain stones. Why do you like them? How do they make you feel? Head out on a field trip to a rock museum or a local quarry.
- Go for a walk in the woods to tap in to the earth's energies. Dowse for water, minerals, or even caves. Make it a fun outing for the whole family.
- When you feel resonance within your body, ask your higher self for more details and expect the answer to come to you.

Resonance is often experienced as the lift in our heart, the bounce in our step, or even a subtle all-over vibration. It is a feeling of deep connectedness.

HEARTGLOW EXERCISES

In this chapter, we have discussed the importance of sound in fostering resonance in the Field of Intuitive Harmony. We do not need to be professional musicians or holistic practitioners to take advantage of sound in healing and communication enhancement for our families. The following exercises help you appreciate sound at an energetic level and bring you farther down the intuitive parenting path.

EXERCISE 7: HEALING TONES

In this exercise, we are going to use toning and chanting to activate the sleeping energies within us. I suggest you do this activity on your own first and then with your children. Following the exercise, please make sure you record your experiences and reflections in your HeartGlow journal. I recommend you integrate healing tones into your life at least once per week.

Begin by finding space in your home where you can do this task uninterrupted for about fifteen minutes. It will feel sort of silly at first to be making sounds without word meaning, yet realize you are activating the intuition of your right brain—you will be less focused on the logical side of the left brain. Feeling silly is a part of it, so have fun.

Wearing comfortable clothing, stand up straight, and begin with the HeartGlow Primer. Put yourself into a relaxed state by standing comfortably with your feet shoulder-width apart and head up, facing forward. Take a few deep breaths, inhaling slowly through your nose and exhaling slowly out your mouth. Allow the frustrations of the day to leave you, floating far out of your mind. Simply relax. Shake loose any body part you feel tension clinging to. Reach up and run your hands through your hair a few times, slightly tugging your hair, as you run your nails across your scalp. Embrace yourself by wrapping your arms snuggly around your body; send yourself love, acceptance, and understanding. Move your hands and arms to a comfortable position on your lap. Slowly take another deep breath. Say aloud or to yourself: "I am Light. I am Peace. I am Love."

We are going to keep it simple and begin with sounds that are familiar to us—vowel sounds. Think of vowels in the English language and the sounds they represent:

A

E

I

O

U

One by one, tone each vowel sound for about twenty seconds. Play around with the volume you use, as if you are turning the knob of a radio—softer, louder, then softer again. Try a few different pitches and hold them. Do not create a song with a sound; we are going for a solid tone held for twenty seconds. Can you feel the vibration of the sound as you create it? Where do you feel it in your body? As you tone each vowel sound, bring your attention to each of your energy centers. Do you feel a sensation in a specific chakra or body part?

Now I would like you to tone *om* or *aum*, attributed by mystics to be the sound or hum of the Universe. It is often used in meditation and yoga practice, connecting us with the primal energy of all that is. Take your time and tone it slowly: *a-u-m*. Let your body be free and loose. If you feel like moving your arms or legs, do so. I have discovered an interesting dance comes over me when I tone in motion. Allow your natural energies to be expressed in their unique way. Continue to tone for several minutes and even longer if you are feeling deeply connected with the process.

It's time to delve even deeper by chanting your own first name. In chanting, we speak or sing similar tones and notes in a rhythmic and repetitive manner. You may be familiar with Buddhist or Gregorian chanting, so feel free to mimic those styles if it helps you to get started. When Raegan is having a tough day with seizures, we often play a chanting CD to relax her and offer sound healing. To begin, simply sing your name slowly, and then sing it slowly in a new way with similar tones. For example, using Raegan's name: "*Raegan ... Rae-A-gan ... Rae-A-A-A-gan*," and so on. There is no limit to the combinations or tones to use. By chanting your own name, you are honoring the deepest aspects of yourself and affirming your connectedness to universal energy. Consider it a portal to falling in love with you! It is an immensely beautiful process that frequently stimulates visualizations and spiritual messages.

After you have experienced toning and chanting for yourself, you can do this exercise again with your children. I find it helpful to have families sit on the floor in a circle. Take turns chanting each other's names. Ask the children how they feel and what they may sense. Remember to have fun with it, as the levity of laughter also facilitates connection to higher vibrations. Write your impressions and experiences in your HeartGlow journal and repeat this exercise as often as you like.

EXERCISE 8: THE SOUND JOURNEY

It's time to take a sound journey. I would like you to select one of your favorite relaxation CDs for this exercise. There are a number of products available intentionally designed to foster balance, tranquility, and healing. You may already have classical or New Age titles in your own collection, which would be appropriate for this activity. Please use a piece that is primarily instrumental, with limited or no lyrics. I would like your creative process to be free to flow, unrestricted by the limitations words sometimes project. It would be fine to use a piece that has animal sounds, such as whales, dolphins, or birds. The choice is yours.

Begin with the HeartGlow Primer. Then while sitting upright and well supported, play the CD in its entirety. You need to be in a relaxed yet alert state. Gently close your eyes to avoid the distraction of the room's visual cues, allowing your hearing and heart to take the lead. We don't want you to fall asleep, so I advise you be sitting instead of lying down. Too many people zone out, begin snoring, and miss out on the entire experience. Contemplate the music as it comes to you. Allow the chords, tones, and energy of the composition to soothe you. Pay close attention to how your body feels. What do you sense in your energy centers? Are any emotions being triggered?

Bring your attention to your mind's eye. Is this beautiful music revealing an image, scene, or memory? Float into the unknown with the sounds. See yourself happy and relaxed, drifting along with the melody. Where have you been brought? What do you see? Continue this journey of sound until the CD ends. When the music is complete, slowly come back to the present moment, bringing your awareness to the room you are in. Wiggle your fingers and toes. Take a few slow, deep breaths and softly open your eyes.

Immediately write your perceptions in your HeartGlow journal. Be specific with your notation by stating your observations and insights physically, mentally, emotionally, and spiritually. Record any and all images you experienced and messages you received. A meditative sound journey such as this is a powerful forum for intuitive communication. You are entering corridors of your soul we often leave unexplored.

When doing this exercise with your children, make appropriate changes to accommodate their age, abilities, and interests. For example, when doing this activity with an infant or very young child, I would snuggle with them or even rock in a chair. Older children may prefer to do this just prior to or after a nap, so lie down with them for a song or two. Adolescents and teenagers can do it just as you would, so sit together and enjoy. It is essential for this to be an endeavor of love, comfort, and exploration. You are not going to get anywhere if you are forcing your kids to participate. Children naturally dance in realms often unfamiliar to us, so take their lead and encourage creative play.

If you are dedicated to enhancing your intuitive skills and increasing resonance with your Field of Intuitive Harmony, do the exercise often with different types of music. Turn off the television; put away the video games and computer for a while. Connect with one another. We are delving into methods that bring us together, not keep us apart.

SUMMARY OF KEY POINTS

Sound therapy is a broad term used to describe a healing modality in which sound or vibration address health conditions in people. These conditions can be physical, emotional, mental, or spiritual in nature and affect those in all walks of life. Originally developed from the work of Dr. Alfred Tomatis, sound therapy has been explored for over fifty years with new discoveries just beginning to be associated with the well-being and balance of our subtle energy systems.

In understanding sound as an energetic modality, one must understand that this creative healing art is an expression of Divine energy. All things in the Universe, including the Universe itself, have a certain vibration and thus a sound. Sound healing presumes that by balancing and harmonizing the vibrations within our physical and auric bodies, healing will naturally occur. This premise leads to a discussion on sound as not only a musical expression but also as a powerful tool of vibration, tones, and frequencies. We have the natural capacity to open our hearts, minds, and bodies to healing sounds.

Clinical research and practical application indicate music therapy facilitates development in sensory, motor, cognitive, and communication skills. It is important to note that these modalities are not limited to the use and application by a certified medical practitioner. Music is being explored in homes and by complementary alternative practitioners to create balance not only in the physical body but also in the chakras and energy fields of clients. The field of vibration therapy is currently being explored by both traditional and alternative practitioners for its unique contribution to health and wellness. An alternative approach in vibration therapy uses the frequencies of a tuning fork or crystal to balance the vibration in the auric field or physical body of a client.

The intuitive healing arts are now gaining scientific validity, which can only lead to additional advancements in study and practice. The amazing correlation yet to be made points to future vibration research expanding the measurement of and attunement to the exact frequency of Divine healing energy. Your resonance with an object or person may offer you a unique opportunity to tap in to Divine energy.

HeartGlow Hints for Intuitive Parenting

- Tone sounds each morning to wake up your energetic sensitivities. Try *oooh* and *aaah* as you and the kids are getting ready for your day.
- Get a drum and find your primal beat. First try this alone and then with your children.
- Take a vow of silence for a day to unlock passages of your soul.
- Appreciate the diverse sounds of nature. Where do you feel them in your body?
- Expand your definition of music by exploring the sounds and celebrations of other cultures. Exposing your children to diversity early on fosters unity, understanding, and creativity, leading to a joyful, vibrant life.

5

The Resonance of Touch

Touch seems to be as essential as sunlight.

DIANE ACKERMAN, *A NATURAL HISTORY OF THE SENSES*

In HeartGlow living, touch is a crucial component to increasing resonance within the Field of Intuitive Harmony and enjoying a healthy, vibrant relationship with our families. A simple hug goes a long way in conveying the heart's emotional and energetic intentions. The powerful therapeutic possibilities of healing touch, whether it is Reiki, laying on of hands, or other methods, can be expanded in practice and further implemented in our homes. Parents and caregivers employing these ancient methods take greater direct responsibility for the health and well-being of themselves and their family. This practice not only significantly reduces the financial burdens on a family but also infuses each family member with knowledge of Divine healing energy, which exists within everyone.

The Touch Research Institute, based at the University of Miami School of Medicine, has been conducting studies into the effects of touch on health since 1992. Although pediatric inquiries have been limited, overall analysis shows clear advantages in healing with touch therapy.[1]

In other research, Michael Cohen indicates pediatricians are integrating the use of alternative therapies, including touch, with chronically ill children. This study goes on to report the need for the medical community to become more aware of these alternative therapies and establish a dialogue with parents on their use.[2] We, however, do not need research to tell us touch feels good. The healing, calming presence of our mother's touch is one of our first experiences on Earth. When you look to the Divine light within you, ask yourself, do you prefer a warm embrace or a cold shoulder?

FOUNDATIONS IN ENERGETIC TOUCH

Barbara Ann Brennan, a pioneer in the field of hands-on healing, introduced the concepts of High Sense Perception and healing the mind, body, and spirit through balancing the human energy field. She refers to the process of this form of energy healing as laying on of hands, faith healing, or spiritual healing. The basic process in a hands-on healing session is quite simple. The client lies on a massage table or comfortable surface, fully clothed with their eyes closed. The client is encouraged by the practitioner to reach a state of relaxation and connectedness to the Universe through deep breathing and intention. This atmosphere allows the healer to better visualize disturbances in the client's auric field and facilitate the balancing of the energy. Divine healing energy channels into the practitioner, then travels through their hands to the client, restoring the aura. The pinnacle of Brennan's theory is the assertion that when the body's energies are in balance, health occurs.[3]

Through spiritual healing touch, the gracious and gentle heart of a healer can assist people in balancing their energy and thus transform their lives. This powerful healing technique is more than a mystical construct or New Age whimsy. Parents have a distinct advantage in healing through energetic touch due to the enhanced connectedness within the Field of Intuitive Harmony. Mounting viable clinical research and ongoing practical applications demonstrate the power behind touch. Developing the parental skills essential to heightened energetic perception is attainable to those who live in truth with their hearts open to the experiences of the world. Overcoming the confines of our egos is a crucial step in intensifying our awareness to the powers of the Universe. This is what we are exploring in Heart-Glow—living with an intuitive heart, open and expansive to the wonderful possibilities that surround us.

In addition to Brennan's energy-based approach to the laying on of hands, history should also be considered. Religions and spiritual organizations throughout the world have been applying forms of Divine touch for centuries. The amazing power of the Almighty has been recognized intuitively to provide comfort and healing to the ill, including children of diverse and varied cultures. The gesture of laying on hands is used in baptisms and other ceremonies and sacraments in Christianity, Judaism, and Spiritualism, among others. Regardless of the specific religion or region of the world, the intention of the power of God moving through the hands of the healer into the faithful is the same.

Diane Stein, author and healing expert, demystifies the ancient art of Reiki and brings its practical application to the Western world. Reiki, which Stein defines as "universal life force energy," can be traced back to India in the days before Jesus.[4] Its history and written record is somewhat in dispute by a variety of religions, as well as its own traditional and nontraditional schools of practice. What is certain is that its reemergence in Japan in the 1800s was ushered in by Mikao Usui, who received knowledge of this ancient healing technique after a twenty-one-day meditation on Mount Koriyama in Japan.

Although the healing methods are quite similar in procedure, the primary difference between Reiki and the method of laying on hands is the belief in and process of attunements. An attunement is an initiation, which creates the healer by passing down energy from master to student. The three levels of Reiki practitioners indicate the ability to channel *ki*, the Japanese word for "energy," from which the term *Reiki* is derived. It is important to note Reiki's focus on the healer as having a power in which only those who have been attuned can harness and those who haven't cannot. At one point in time, Reiki attunements and treatments were primarily for the wealthy and elite. Fortunately now, healers and educators such as Stein have been breaking down those barriers by opening the world of Reiki to all interested in exploring it.

The use and true understanding of Reiki in the United States, however, has been quite limited. It is widely known and implemented in holistic and spiritual centers, yet in traditional care environments it can be found only in small numbers of progressive chronic-care facilities and surgical recovery units. In its partnership with allopathic environments, Reiki is often thought of only as a means for relaxation to manage anxiety and moderate pain, as opposed to an actual method of energetic healing.

Philip Chan, a medical doctor and Reiki practitioner, highlights his recommendations to conventional healthcare practitioners in an article for the International Center for Reiki Training. Although a believer in the power of Reiki healing, Chan strongly urges practitioners to refer to the treatment as a "nontraditional bioenergetic system of stress relief" and advocates a non-touch approach to avoid accusations of misconduct.[5] The spiritual nature of this modality is clearly not explored by this interpretation, which appears to be dictated by the allopathic medical establishment's fear and limitations. Surely, Divine healing energy can transcend the self-imposed limits of the human ego, surpassing the meager expectations of conventional medicine.

In his research on Reiki in hospitals, Hans Van Leeuwen reports the U.S. government's growing interest in researching the benefits of complementary alternative therapies due to patients' dissatisfaction with conventional medicine, which no longer addressed their "values, beliefs, and philosophical orientations toward health and life."[6] This added interest by the administration could pave a new way of looking at Reiki and remove the shackles of skepticism and limitation on its application. It is apparent that patients desire a higher level of care, one which addresses their specific wants not only physically but also mentally, emotionally, and spiritually.

A DOCTOR'S MAGIC TOUCH

Raegan and I were becoming regulars at the hospital in Boston. The recovery regimen from the surgical error involved repeated procedures to dilate her esophagus just above her stomach in hopes of opening the area, which had been restricted by the stitch. Stabilized from the initial problems, we were able to go home and make only short trips back for the dilatations. These procedures were not as drastic as everything else she had already gone through, yet there was still risk involved in them, including undergoing anesthesia. Although we hoped she would one day be able to eat by mouth again, our primary goal was to improve her ability to swallow saliva and basically be more comfortable in her daily life.

Always staying in the same surgical ward, we became quite close to a number of the nurses and staff members who worked there. In fact, a few of them would come in to visit us on their day off if they knew Raegan was going to be there. Getting increasingly comfortable in the environment, Mark and I even looked forward to our favorite buffalo chicken wraps in the cafeteria and knew of places around the corner to duck out to for some head space.

Our sweet girl handled her hospitalizations with an adventurous spirit, making it easier for us to cope with our own emotional baggage. Having met so many wonderful families there for different treatments, we relished in witnessing their personal triumphs. In truth, I never before realized the variety and magnitude of illnesses children face. It simply didn't occur to me. Raegan, herself, was a blossom that had come back to life due to the care and nurturing of the loving gardeners we encountered.

Waiting in the noisy pre-op room just prior to one of her procedures, I held Raegan's hand as Mark made silly voices to distract her from discomfort. She was thrashing a bit, alert and agitated from the newly placed IV in her arm. We would soon be seeing her off to surgery, but first we needed to go through all the necessary steps to get her ready. It seemed like dozens of different people in surgical garb stopped by to read her chart, all with a unique interest or question regarding their involvement in the procedure. The room was filled with other children all going through the same intake process, their anxious parents also trying to remain calm. Raegan was not appreciating the frenetic energy of the room and was beginning to struggle with it all. "Not much longer Angel-Baby," I said as I stroked her soft, curly hair.

"Good morning, lovely lady," said a handsome man in blue scrubs as he walked up to Raegan's bed. He was talking directly to her, giving Mark and me a wink and a smile. "I'm your date for the morning and will make sure you're relaxed and comfortable for your procedure today," he said as he placed one hand near the top of her head. Continuing to explain his role to her as the anesthesiologist, he began subtly moving his hands just above her in a slight sweeping motion. So subtle, most would not have noticed. Never taking his eyes or attention away from Raegan, he explained to us—by talking to her—which medications he would administer and precisely what he would be monitoring. Occasionally, he would gently touch her head, arm, or foot. Raegan's anxiety lessened as she soaked in the luxurious sound of his voice, her muscles no longer fighting the IV.

"What's he doing—using energy?" Mark whispered to me under his breath.

"I think he is," I replied softly, continuing to watch the doctor's every move. There was something unusual, yet somehow familiar, at work here. Slightly closing my eyes, I felt my mind immediately flood with intense colors—blue, pink, orange, and gold. The dancing hues swirled and swayed in front of me, as the soft yet steady voice of the healer lifted me higher. Feeling as if I were being embraced by a sunrise, I felt my heart center gently open like a flower. As I glided into the energetic bliss, my own hesitations and concerns floated away. It was all so beautiful.

Slowly refocusing my attention back to the room, I could see my daughter was now peacefully sleeping from the gentle urgings of energetic touch. Requiring no medical sedation to relax her, she was ready to be wheeled into the operating room. "Don't worry, Mom and Dad," the doctor said, walking beside Rae's bed as it pulled away from us. Encapsulated by a wash of light, they slowly made their way past screaming children and noisy machines. Stunned, I began to wonder if I was crazy or had imagined the whole thing.

"Wow, I've never seen anything like it," Mark said in amazement. Apparently, we shared the delusion.

Just then, a nurse pleasantly walked up, ready to escort us to the waiting room.

"Does he do that all the time?" I asked, nodding toward the anesthesiologist as they headed toward the operating room.

"He's an amazing doctor," was her only reply.

It was as though we all knew miracles were happening right before our eyes, yet we weren't supposed to mention it. Gathering our belongings and following her out of the room, Mark and I felt blessed to have witnessed such an occurrence and even more blessed that Raegan was under his care.

The procedure went extremely well. Raegan recovered quickly and required no additional medication for pain or seizures, which often increased with the stress of surgery. In fact, she seemed to come out of the surgical haze sooner than with previous procedures. The magic touch of a doctor was not magic at all. He was a master of energy and intention, utilizing a healing touch with his other traditional medical skills. Demonstrating a hybrid of beliefs—not choosing one over the other—he was incorporating both traditional and energetic methods to be an optimum healer. Although we had no concrete evidence of our suspicions, our own empirical data was beginning to mount. Whether we are aware of it or not, energy plays an enormous role in our lives. Through expanding our perspectives and honoring our connections, we increase our energy awareness and activate our intuitive hearts.

A PARENT'S INTUITIVE TOUCH

Everybody needs a hug.
It changes your metabolism.

—LEO BUSCAGLIA

Cami, one of my clients, is mother to a child with cerebral palsy. One day she was called home from work when her daughter would not stop crying. Taking her to the emergency room, doctors began to run tests to see what might be wrong. Holding her daughter close to calm her, Cami heard an internal voice say: "Check the left foot." Slowly she removed her daughter's sock, revealing swelling and a large bruise. Upon questioning her school caretakers, it was discovered the child's foot had gotten pinched when she was transferred onto the bus earlier in the day. The driver did not realize the little girl had been injured. Later, when the foot began to swell in her shoe, the child's pain and tears began.

"I was thrilled to get such a specific message. I didn't know I could do it!" Cami told me with excitement. In this instance, a mother's loving touch was not only soothing for her child but also led to a vital discovery.

Research supports what we innately understand; our connection to those we love heals and can be strengthened further by the intimacy of touch. Think back to the miraculous, energetic feelings stirred within you when you held hands with your first love or cradled your newborn baby. Touch accurately conveys the energy and intentions of our soul. Loving touch expands us, as warmth emanates from the heart and palm centers. Touch through anger contracts, closing us off from the Divine flow and those around us. We must be aware of how we physically interact with others and take responsibility for the energy we are creating in our relationships. The passage to peace and wholeness is illuminated by the grace of a loving caress.

Parents have a unique attunement to their families due to proximity, genetic signature, and loving intent. Our healing capacity can exceed the methods of a Reiki master if we simply utilize our natural bonds to one another. The power of energetic touch is available to us, should we choose to employ it. Focusing our attention on how we touch one another—physically, emotionally, and energetically—is vital to intuitive parenting. Keep these simple touch activities in mind as you try to increase resonance with your family:

- Hold hands, cuddle, or snuggle. When you touch one another, have love in your heart.

- Take the time to explore an energy healing session with your family. It can work wonders with headaches, anxiety, and overall wellness.
- Be mindful of your intentions. Exude what you desire. Do not expect closeness when you are the one putting up the barriers.
- Stop any aggressive movements and touch. *Do not* spank, hit, or smack. This behavior conveys harmful energy—even more than you know.
- Dance together. The combination of music and touch is a fun way to raise the vibration and exchange energy.

HEARTGLOW TOUCH TECHNIQUES

Appreciating the energetic benefits of touch at its highest level is achieved through dedication and commitment. Incorporating activities with your family and being mindful of our actions can lead to dramatic improvements in all aspects of living. The following touch techniques are for parents who wish to take their energetic connections with their children to the next level. These particular methods have been used with children of all ages and developmental ability levels. They can be done when the child is awake or sleeping, standing or lying down, and are designed to be incorporated into a busy life. Start with only five-minute sessions and increase the time frame as you become more comfortable with the techniques.

THE HEARTGLOW TENDER TOUCH

1. Clear and balance your own energy field prior to reaching out, so as not to pass along any clouded energy to your family member. You can use the HeartGlow Primer to begin and continue with the Aura Wash technique from chapter 2.

2. Take a breath and bring your attention to your heart center. Slowly begin to magnify your heart's glow by thinking loving, caring thoughts. Feel the Divine energy rise within you.

3. Set your intentions for healing, peace, communication, and love.

4. Focus awareness on your palm centers. The energy will begin to flow through you.

5. In a slow, deliberate manner, reach out and touch your loved one at their heart center. Feeling the energy flow between you, send your love and any message you would like to convey. If you are then guided to move to another energy center, do so slowly.

6. Be open to anything you receive. End the session with a deep breath, expressing gratitude to the Universe.

THE HEARTGLOW HOVER: THE "DO NOT TOUCH" TOUCH

1. Clear and balance your own energy field prior to reaching out, so as not to pass along clouded energy to your family member.

2. Take a breath and bring your attention to your heart center. Slowly begin to magnify your heart's glow by thinking loving, caring thoughts. Feel the Divine energy rise within you.

3. Set your intentions for healing, peace, communication, and love.

4. Focus awareness on your palm centers. The energy will begin to flow through you.

5. In a slow, deliberate manner, reach out toward your loved one. Place your hands approximately two to three inches away from them, hovering above them.

6. Using all your sensitivities, move along their body, tuning in to their energetic field and energy centers. If it helps, close your eyes to bring forth information from your more subtle senses.

7. Make note of any cues you receive. It is essential you look beyond your own ego filters to make room for Divine guidance and healing. When your session is complete, take a deep breath and express gratitude for the experience.

The HeartGlow touch techniques are beneficial for parents desiring a higher level of communication with their children, especially if traditional verbal exchange is limited. You are opening yourself to an energetic dialogue, an entirely new way of sharing information. Be open to how this information may come to you. One mother of a child with autism was thrilled to see her son not only enjoying the HeartGlow touch sessions but also asking for them by placing her hand on his chest when she was preparing him for bed. It is now a special ritual they share, and she was thrilled to report she is beginning to understand his energetic messages. Energetic touch is a compelling component in your intuitive parenting toolbox.

When beginning energy healing in your home, it can be beneficial to also consult a professional energy practitioner as a form of backup. One unique method of energetic touch therapy we have incorporated into Raegan's routine is called Chi Reisage. Suzanne Silvermoon, a holistic nurse and yoga master, has developed this technique to address the numerous and diverse needs of the pediatric community she services.

In her sessions with Raegan, Suzanne utilizes healing stones, music, and touch as well as visualization and prayer to address any imbalances she perceives. Suzanne's support and feedback on Raegan's energetic health is a valuable contribution to our family, as it keeps us on track. We have been encouraged by the consistency of the energetic messages we each receive from Raegan. Being able to compare notes, so to speak, allows us to be confident in understanding Raegan's communication.

HeartGlow Exercises

We have learned in this chapter the importance of touch in fostering resonance in the Field of Intuitive Harmony. We need not be a Reiki master to succeed, as our own connections within our families give us an enhanced opportunity for healing and communication. These next two touch exercises allow you to demonstrate your newfound intuitive parenting wisdom.

Exercise 9: The Energy Wave

In this exercise, you will learn to use an energetic wave to provide comfort to your children. This activity is for you to do as a treatment for your children and can even be done when they are sleeping.

I use the energy wave technique with Raegan when she is especially restless or trying to get over an illness. If she is awake at the time, she will often get the giggles as she is enjoying the wave of energy washing over her. HeartGlow parents have reported this to be especially helpful with tantrums and moods swings in their children. At a minimum, consider doing the energy wave monthly as a preventative tool. Following the exercise, please make sure you record your experiences and reflections in your HeartGlow journal.

Prepare yourself with the HeartGlow Primer. To begin the energy wave, have your child lay on their bed in a relaxed manner. This is a great exercise to do just prior to sleep, so having them comfy in their pajamas will only help. You can choose to play relaxing music in the background if it helps you connect with your healing energies. Be open with your child about this being an energy exercise and encourage his/her involvement based on their age and development. I do recommend performing this during sleep for smaller children, as they tend not to settle down into a relaxed state. If you are doing this exercise with a teen, have him/her read the instructions, so they know what to expect in the session, and encourage them to give you an energy wave session the next night.

With your child lying in bed, stand beside them and take a few deep breaths. Encourage your child to relax and close their eyes. If he/she is already asleep—perfect. Set your intention for peace and healing. Close your eyes and visualize your child's energy field with your subtle senses. How large is it? What colors do you see? What do you feel? Is there anything in particular which draws your attention within their aura?

Stretch your arms and hands in front of you, hovering over your child. Bring your hands to approximately six inches above their body. Take a deep breath as you begin to feel your energy fields intertwine. Starting at the top of their head, sweep your outstretched arms and hands down their body. Do this slowly at first in one motion, just like a wave. When you get to the bottom of their feet, slide your arms downward and begin again at the top. Slightly increase your speed as you continue the energy wave again and again. Feel the momentum building as you ride the flow of energy. Refrain from projecting your own wants and desires while in this state, as it will constrain the flow. Simply exude love and peace. Although the energy is moving through you, it comes directly from the Divine source.

After a few moments, reduce your speed and begin to wind the exercise down. Say a prayer of gratitude and call your own energy back to yourself. Take a few slow breaths and gently open your eyes, returning to the present moment. Make note of your experiences in your HeartGlow journal for reflection at a later time. The next day, ask your child for their feedback, if he/she was an active participant with you.

This level of energetic closeness can be awkward for some at first, so please be patient with yourself as you develop your energy sensitivities. Many people discover old wounds they never completely processed, so be kind to yourself if emotional issues crop up. Do not rush yourself or your child. If any HeartGlow exercise is uncomfortable for you to do, let it go for now and try again another time.

EXERCISE 10: POINT TO POINT

In this next exercise, I want you to explore the energy centers of yourself and your child. Specifically, how you sense the energy points in each other through touch. This activity can be done when your child is awake or asleep. If you really want to have fun with it, make it a game for the entire family to participate in— even your pets. Yes, they have energy centers too!

Please feel free to refer back to the chart in chapter 2 for energy center points. Although the approximate body locations of the major chakras have been documented for centuries, there can be slight variations. Highly sensitive people can often detect the various minor centers as well, so do not be alarmed if you discover additional centers in alternate places on the body. There are immense volumes focusing solely on the study of the chakras for you to investigate further if you desire a deeper spiritual understanding of the system. I have included a suggested reading list at the back of this book.

Start by finding your own palm centers. Shake out your hands and wiggle your fingers. Rotate your wrists and flex your arms. Gently rub your hands together, and then hold them palm up in front of you. Close your eyes and visualize the gems at the center of your palms glowing brightly. How does this feel to you? Do you notice a twinge, heat, or coolness coming from your palm centers? Some describe it as a tickle or vibration, which in fact is a subtle vibration. Hold your palms facing each other about three inches apart. Slowly move your hands in and out, as if you were almost clapping. Move your hands in a circular motion, as if you were rolling a ball of dough. Can you feel the sensation of your own energy field? Keep working with this until you can sense the energy between your hands. This step needs to be understood before you move on, as we will be sensing the other energy points with our palm centers for this exercise.

When you are ready to move on, copy the following chart in your HeartGlow journal, leaving room for your own comments. Include a column for yourself and each child you are doing this exercise with.

Energy Center	My Child	Myself
Heart center		
Throat center		
Third eye center		

Now starting with the heart center, place your palm about six inches in front of your child's chest. You are opening yourself up to sense the energy of his or her heart center. Just as you did with your own hands, move your hand closer to and away from their body. Close your eyes if it helps you to activate your more subtle senses. What do you feel? A temperature? A pressure? An emotion? Where is it? Does it change size? Take it all in and write your impressions in your HeartGlow journal. Repeat this same step for the throat center and third eye. Make sure to note how these centers differ from one another. When you are finished, do the same exploration on yourself. How do your own energy centers feel?

You can do this for all seven major centers, if you wish. However, I recommend breaking it up into several smaller sessions, as children often lose interest quickly and you begin to fight the current. We're all about going with the flow, so when you feel resistance, let go. No two experiences are ever the same, so do not compare children or judge someone's energy flow as right or wrong. In fact, in this exercise, we are not attempting to heal or change anything; we are discovering. This is a learning activity to begin to understand how energy is processed in your child and self at that particular moment.

I have witnessed my own daughter's energy go to extremes and have learned she knows exactly what she is doing for herself. Had I intervened by attempting to alter her processing, I could have done more harm than good. Basically, I am saying that each of our energetic systems knows best. Do not allow your fears or worries to get in the way of your child's internal Divine guidance. It is difficult not to project our needs or desires, yet realize we are merely a conduit for the energy. Our bias can alter the purity of the flow. This can be a hang-up even for professional healers, who get attached to a certain outcome. Remember to assist your child energetically; sincerely send them love from your heart center. Love is the highest form of energy we know and the language we speak. Our next chapter delves further into the depths of the resonance of love.

SUMMARY OF KEY POINTS

Touch is a crucial component to increasing resonance within the Field of Intuitive Harmony and enjoying a healthy, vibrant relationship with our families. A simple hug goes a long way in conveying the heart's emotional and energetic intentions. Parents and caregivers employing these ancient methods take greater direct responsibility for the health and well-being of themselves and their family. This practice not only significantly reduces the financial burdens on a family but also infuses them with knowledge of Divine healing energy, which exists within everyone. Through spiritual healing touch, the gracious and gentle heart of a healer can assist clients in balancing their energy, and thus transform their lives.

Religions and spiritual organizations throughout the world have been applying forms of Divine touch for centuries. The gesture of laying on hands is used in baptisms and ceremonies and sacraments in Christianity, Judaism, and Spiritualism, among others. Parents have a distinct advantage in healing through energetic touch due to the enhanced connectedness within the Field of Intuitive Harmony. Mounting, viable clinical research and ongoing practical applications demonstrate the power behind touch. Developing the parental skills essential to heightened energetic perception is attainable to those who live in truth with their hearts open to the experiences of the world. Overcoming the confines of our egos is a crucial step in intensifying our awareness to the powers of the Universe.

Loving touch expands us. Touch through anger contracts, closing us off from the Divine flow and those around us. Parents have a unique attunement to their families due to proximity, genetic signature, and loving intent. Bringing our attention and intention to how we touch one another physically, emotionally, and energetically is crucial to intuitive parenting. Appreciating the energetic benefits of touch at its highest level is achieved through dedication and commitment. Incorporating activities with your family and being mindful of our actions can lead to dramatic improvements in all aspects of living.

HeartGlow Hints for Intuitive Parenting

- A tender touch heals, awakens, and celebrates the Spirit.
- Massage hands and feet with a soothing lotion or oil to relieve tension and activate energy centers.
- Think back to those whose physical touch has affected you. Why was the connection significant? What emotions did you feel?
- Realize touch is a powerful conveyer of energy and a beacon to truth.
- Take the time to embrace those you love. Do this with complete awareness and clarity of heart and mind to truly be present in the moment.

6

The Resonance of Love

Your task is not to seek for love, but merely to seek and find all the barriers within yourself that you have built against it.

A COURSE IN MIRACLES

Mystics, poets, and spiritual practitioners throughout the centuries have been saying the same three words: "God is Love." The Divine Essence is the source and expression of all love in the Universe. Learning, demonstrating, and celebrating love within us is the purpose of life itself. This amazing power of love can be clearly represented in the life journey of our families. Parents are in the unique position of being on the giving and receiving end of pure, unconditional love. The world has no better display of grace than a parent caring for their child and the child—vulnerable and ever trusting in the parent's care—demonstrating great faith, peace, and reliance on the Almighty.

The Universe provides daily opportunities for the expression of love to everyone. Each of us has individual relationships, interactions, and experiences that bestow prospects for allowing our loving God light to shine. The choice is ours through our actions and intentions whether we live in the expansion of love or in the limitation of fear—deciding for ourselves if we want a life based on freedom and peace, or on control and manipulation. The healing radiance of love flows through all beings yet can be restricted by our inattention to the vibration and lack of knowledge of the process.

What is Love? We talk about it all the time, but what do we really know it to be? A feeling? A responsibility? An energy? It is all those things—and more. The following definition, put forth by the Institute for Research on Unlimited Love, is by far the most beautiful statement on the intricacies and energies associated with love:

> The essence of love is to affectively affirm as well as to unselfishly delight in the well-being of others, and to engage in acts of care and service on their behalf; unlimited love extends this love to all others without exception, in an enduring and constant way. Widely considered the highest form of virtue, unlimited love is often deemed a Creative Presence underlying and integral to all of reality: participation in unlimited love constitutes the fullest experience of spirituality.[1]

If this is the definition of love you live by, congratulations. It is what I strive for each day, yet I admit I often fall short of it due to limitations imposed by my ego and childhood programming. Be patient with yourself; we are all beautiful, energetic works in progress.

Our relationships with our children are often the most sincere form of love we experience in our lives, a perfect example of how we should approach love with others. Why is it that we can love our children without limits but have trouble applying this same belief to everyone? Simply put, we resonate with our children at a higher level, so the love and energy flows purely. Think of it as an inherent resonance—Momma or Poppa Bear's innate urgings to care for and protect their cub. Although we love our other life partners, we have had to build the resonance in those relationships over a period of time, with great effort and intention. When our interest or focus on the relationship changes, the energy of love can dissipate, as it has no inherent resonance to support it. We can feel out of sync with our kids yet do not file for a parental divorce.

Most of us have become complacent with the expectations, projections, and rules for controlling interpersonal relationships, which we are misguided into believing is love. Primarily, society's understanding of love is inaccurate and based on conditional circumstances and behaviors: you do what I want; I'll do what you want; then we will love each other. We are often taught to judge, compete, and control, when it comes to affairs of the heart. Our culture's current obsession with reality television is a perfect example of this limited view of love and behavior, which is then compounded and further exploited by the media. I assure you, this mediated reality speaks the language of agenda promotion and money, not unlimited love.

Myopic perceptions of love are outside of the Divine Self and do not consider the virtuous universal vibration within us. We need to challenge ourselves to move beyond a meager perspective and expand our definition of love to encompass all. Recognize in everyone the inherent resonance we have for our children. We are each a part of the same Creative Presence of Love—a vibrant, inclusive force, not an exclusive club reserved only for those who behave in a certain manner, wear particular clothing, or donate a portion of their salary. By raising our children with the conscious awareness of God love energy, we shift our world into a new realm of peace and a time of transcendence for all.

CHANNELS OF LOVE

Sitting in the living room of our home in Maine, I looked up at the patterns of the tin ceiling, lost in thought over the past year's events.

Another winter was now upon us, which seemed to spur a sense of melancholy and contemplation in me. Raegan was now four years old. We had recently returned home after another dilatation procedure in Boston, the twelfth surgery in Raegan's young life. The procedures had accomplished their goal of allowing her to swallow secretions and be more comfortable. Things were looking up.

Thrilled to be home again, we were getting back into the routine of life. Nursing services assisted us with Raegan's daily care. Having decided to go back to school to study metaphysics, I was running a small spiritual gift shop from my home. This allowed me to be with Raegan, advance my studies, and also welcome new people and experiences into my life.

On this particular day, Raegan seemed anxious, and I asked our nurse, Gloria, to keep a close eye on her. Speaking to the doctors by phone, we were told to keep watching and to bring her in if she got worse. Our concerns grew with every moment as Raegan began to thrash in discomfort. Suddenly, an ear-piercing scream cut through the air as Raegan curled into a ball and rolled onto her side. Rushing to her, we debated calling an ambulance. Then as quickly as she yelled out, Raegan relaxed and fell asleep. Her vital signs stable, I thought maybe she had severe gas pain, like she'd had countless times before.

"I don't like it," Gloria said strongly. "You get her to the hospital if anything seems off," she continued as she hesitantly left for the day.

Raegan remained quiet and peaceful. She looked so adorable sleeping soundly in the middle of Mommy's bed. There was no obvious indication anything might be wrong with her. However, my body again began to quake. Hands shaking and teeth chattering, I was trying to get a grip on the situation. Mark and I frantically searched for any clue that something was out of the ordinary with our girl, not exactly an easy thing to do when her baseline was so compromised. Our "normal" was far from normal. The three of us cuddled close in our bed all night—Raegan sleeping soundly while we lay awake watching her.

When the sun rose the next morning, I sighed deeply, wondering why my body still had me on high alert. Reaching down to check Raegan's stomach tube and start her breakfast, my worst fears became realized. Viscous green bile was backing up into her stomach, just as we'd seen before when she had an intestinal blockage. Something was wrong! "Mark, please call an ambulance," I said with intense calm. He flew to the phone without asking a question, sensing the urgency in my voice. We quickly dressed and waited for the first responders.

In a town of less than five thousand people, Raegan was well-known to most of the emergency workers. Taking her vitals and listening to my report, they transferred her into the ambulance as I climbed into the back beside them and Mark followed in the car behind us.

Sitting in the back of the ambulance, my body and mind had become eerily still, while my senses magnified every little sight and sound. I smiled at Raegan, who was flirting with the paramedic as he struggled to get an IV into a very jumpy, bumpy girl who was thrashing about. Through the vehicle's small back window, I could see Mark directly behind us. The lines on his face appeared especially deep this morning as he concentrated on his driving.

The staff was waiting for us when we arrived at the emergency room. The ER physician immediately got on the phone with her specialists in Boston and rushed Raegan into the X-ray room. Within minutes, he came up to us and handed me a large envelope with the X-ray inside. "They are expecting you in Boston," he said. Looking to him to explain the results to me, I began to ask a question. He put his hand on my shoulder and said, "You need to go now. They'll explain it to you there."

Piling into the ambulance, I looked back to see the line of emergency room workers watching closely to make sure we were on our way. Seeing a tear form in the eye of one of the nurses, I knew our situation was grave. "Oh, AngelBaby," I said, looking down at Raegan, taking her hand and softly kissing it. Groggy from a dose of medication, she was snuggled up in her blankets and falling back to sleep. She showed no fear or anxiety, even though her color was becoming a bit ashen and blotchy. Dialing my mother on my cell phone, I sat back to prepare for the long ride. Even in a high-speed ambulance, it would take three hours to get there. Mark was speeding directly behind us. I could see him setting his jaw to face what was to come—whatever that was.

Arriving in Boston, a member of the surgical team was waiting for us when we walked inside. He explained that Raegan's doctor was at a conference out of town and had personally asked him to care for her. He was to bring her immediately into a swallow study, as the X-rays had revealed a perforation, not the intestinal blockage we had first suspected.

Going in for the study, Raegan was alert and smiling. Yet the doctor explained the results to me—a severe bacterial infection, which had come from the perforation of her esophagus. The rupture could not be repaired surgically, and they did not expect her to make it through the night. He continued to explain it wouldn't be long before her body would begin to shut down. The green bile backing into her stomach was already a sign of things changing. They would treat Raegan with an aggressive course of antibiotics and allow us to be alone as a family.

Feeling as if every breath had been knocked from my body, I turned away from the doctor. Hearing Mark and Raegan playing joyfully in the hall, I could not imagine how I was going to find the words to tell him this. Hesitantly, I walked toward them, reaching out for their hands, and I gently began to deliver the medical assessment to Mark. Speaking slowly and deliberately, I informed him of what I had just been told. Mark swallowed hard and began to kiss our girl on the neck again. She laughed in delight as we merely tried to breathe.

Waiting in the corridor for our room upstairs, we were in shock and could not express much emotion. Feeling powerless, I placed a call to my friend Sue in an attempt to cope with what was before me. Sue Yarmey was my spiritual adviser and first mentor in studying subtle energies. She had become very dear to my family, understanding Raegan energetically from their first meeting. Sue didn't look at Raegan as disabled. Listening intently to me over the phone, she allowed me to go over all the details of the situation.

"Deb, just because there is nothing they can do doesn't mean there is nothing we can do. This is Raegan's choice. We will give her our love, and she will do what is best for her soul's journey," she explained. Deciding to start a healing prayer circle, we called our friends and fellow energy practitioners, requesting their light and loving intentions for Raegan. The circle's energy could be used to assist Raegan to heal her wounds or facilitate her flight to Heaven; the choice was hers.

After a bit of waiting and scurrying about, the doctor got us settled into a private room in the intensive care unit. Raegan had drifted to sleep peacefully, and I began to wonder if she would wake again. Would I be blessed to see her brilliant smile or hear her joyful laugh another day? Sitting on a rocking chair in the room, I stared blankly at the floor while Mark stood behind me, holding on to my shoulders. The doctor humbly knelt in front of us, as if he were at an altar. "It's in God's hands now," he said. Tear-filled eyes conveyed his sincerity and true sorrow he felt for us. He tenderly held my hands on my knees and stayed with us for a moment in silence. Standing to leave the room, he said, "I'm here for you. Just have me paged and I'll be back." The doctor's intelligence, professionalism, and sincere efforts had been constantly assisting us all day; now his energy was also joining our loving prayer circle.

About an hour later, a nurse walked in the room and said softly, "You have a visitor." Because we were hours from home, in the middle of a winter storm, and the time was getting extremely late, I had no idea who it could be. Looking up, I could see my friend Kathy walk into the room, rushing to embrace me. Her daughter, Natalie, shared Raegan's rare disorder and had passed away the prior year after a long illness.

"I lied and said I was your sister," she said as she hugged me tight.

"You didn't lie," I cried, burying my head into her shoulder, tears flowing freely for the first time.

"They won't let me stay, but I needed you to know all the AngelBabyMoms are praying for you," she said.

AngelBabyMoms is an online support group I had started a few years before.[2] We are a group of mothers of disabled children from all over the world coming together to share the experiences of our lives—now the other moms were sharing their love and support with my family. I knew Kathy's hugs were from them all, their arms stretching out across the globe to hold us in a loving, healing embrace. Stopping at Rae's bedside to give her a kiss, Kathy was honoring the spirit of her own daughter as she tenderly prayed with mine. Their family had already been to the place we now traveled to. Rising to her feet, she wiped her eyes, blew me a kiss, and quickly walked out the door.

The night was long and quiet. Mark and I flanked Raegan's bed, not wanting to be more than a step away from her. The nurse came in from time to time with another large dose of antibiotics. Raegan did not move and her respiration had slowed significantly. Unable to rest at all, I sat beside my daughter visualizing the three of us floating together in space, doing a sort of cosmic dance. I could see the glow of our prayer circle surrounding us, growing larger each moment, as the loving intentions of people joined in the dance. Comforted by the visions of their energy, I realized no matter what happened, it would be as it should be.

"What a beautiful smile!" a voice said brightly. Opening my eyes to a sun-streaked room, I could see the nurse standing over Raegan's bed, smiling down on her. Turning my head slowly toward my daughter, I could see she was not only awake but also grinning from ear to ear. "I think you are going to be able to leave intensive care," said the nurse encouragingly. "It looks like she beat the infection. The doctor will be in shortly to talk with you."

"Not ready to leave us, darling girl?" I asked Raegan with a slight quiver in my voice. She looked at me with a sly grin and sparkling eyes, as if she had discovered the secret to the Universe. In fact, I knew she had.

When the doctor came in later to evaluate her, he was absolutely astounded. Raegan's pinhole perforation had self sealed in the night and was no longer leaking into her chest cavity. The infection was still present but had improved dramatically with the high doses of medication—and love. A few weeks' course of IV antibiotics and she should be fine. "Little girl, you are responsible for half the gray hairs on my head," the doctor said playfully. "I don't know what to tell you. I was arranging grief counseling for you folks. She is extremely resilient."

And so it was. We stayed a few more days in the hospital, followed by IV antibiotics to be administered at home. Raegan had made the choice to stay on the earth with us. It humbles me to realize she could have just as easily chosen to fly to Heaven, like others before her and since. The resonance of love created by the prayer circle made room for miracles to happen. Raegan used the energy to heal, continuing her life as a beacon of hope and possibility for everyone. My daughter is a wonderful example of Divine energy working flawlessly in life—the perfection in imperfection, teaching us all that we are brilliant creatures of love.

HEALING WITH LOVE

Globally, we are beginning to wake up to the healing potential of our intrinsic loving nature. As Deepak Chopra reminds us, "love bonds you to the rhythm of the universe."[3] This bond emanates through us and is demonstrated through our empathy, gratitude, and service to others. It is we who must actively tap into our own relationship to the Divine through our connection and awareness to facilitate healing through love. By choosing to live in love, we expand our perceptions beyond the isolated self and welcome the concept of Universal Oneness into our lives.

Implementing love as a healing therapy is just emerging into our culture in alternative medical settings. According to futurist and social architect August Jaccaci, "we are now beginning to understand that the benevolent use of spirit in our lives is the next stage of human evolution."[4] What a spectacular place for us to be! We are at the dawn of a new way of looking at love in our world. The techniques of meditation, creative visualization, and affirmations are illustrated here for their ability to strengthen love as a healing practice, foster resonance in the Field of Intuitive Harmony, and facilitate deeper individual connections with the Divine. By taking these next steps forward, we empower our society to unleash the healing loving vibration within us all, creating a life of unlimited possibilities for our children.

MEDITATION

Meditation is an exercise of connecting with the Divine Energy through deep relaxation and the absence of active thought. It is the process of quieting the mind to expand awareness and break loose from the bonds of mental and emotional attachments. Meditation is often associated with Eastern religions and philosophies, such as Buddhism, Hinduism, and Yogic traditions. The practice is now expanding into the whole-health movement, not only addressing conditions such as anxiety, pain, and depression, but also balancing the subtle energy systems of our families.

A team of researchers led by psychologist Jean L. Kristeller explored the role of meditation in cultivating love, compassion, kindness, and altruism in our culture. They determined that the systematic tool of meditation suspends the normal process of judgmental thought and leads to greater promotion of empathy, compassion, and spiritual growth. The research further concluded that "meditation . . . can be considered a powerful means of shifting one's relationship to one's own mind, of uncoupling conditioned reactions that may have outlived their time and value, and opening the mind to qualities of experience that create new meaning, wisdom, and love."[5] This is crucial to developing an expansive, love-based modality of healing, which can implement a new protocol in the management of physical, mental, and spiritual well-being.

Our families can significantly benefit from the practice of meditation through its fundamental advantages of peace, clarity of mind, pain management, and stress reduction. The daily responsibilities and burdens that confront most families are often magnified when those families also living with chronic illness or disability. Parents and children alike can use meditation to shift focus from their individual challenges to a loving perspective of universal connectedness. The idea of being one with the All provides immense comfort to those who feel alone, misunderstood, and overwhelmed by life's journey.

The practice of meditation is straightforward and convenient to implement in a home, medical, or spiritual setting and can be done individually or in a group. There are countless books, websites, and CDs which demonstrate numerous and alternative methods of the procedure. Aligning yourself with the Divine energy for only fifteen minutes a day is all that is needed to renew yourself: mind, body, and spirit. Meditation is free, uncomplicated, and portable, an indispensable tool of love to enhance both allopathic and holistic forms of healing.

CREATIVE VISUALIZATION

Creative visualization is a technique that utilizes the power of the imagination to manifest balance and healing in life. This practice can be used to address disorders on all levels of existence. In her pioneering book *Creative Visualization*, Shakti Gawain instructs on the process of using the imagination to bring about all things desired through creating an image, feeling, or idea in your mind, then focusing positive energy toward it until it becomes a reality. The fundamental foundation of this method is the idea of working with the mind to heal the human energy system, therefore addressing illness and disease which had previously developed in the body.

Creative visualization can be implemented in an endless variety of settings and used to work with a myriad of disorders. Both traditional medical and alternative care practitioners utilize forms of visualization in assisting their clients. By imagining only health, well-being, and balance in your life, you can reduce pain and ease anxiety. Paint your life's portrait with the colors and moods you find calming and nurturing. Your own intuitive guidance system will lead the way to creating a picture that will restore your body to its ultimate state of being. This is a powerful technique to put into practice with children, as they are masters of imagination and accustomed to the world of creativity.

Families from all walks of life can deeply benefit from this method, as it simultaneously addresses concerns and conditions in both the child and the parent. A mother caring for a son with cancer can take the child on a beautiful healing journey of imagination with a colorful narrative focusing on joy, love, and fun. This process not only benefits the recovering patient by balancing energy, reducing pain, and easing symptoms, but also heals the storyteller by infusing peace and minimizing anxiety over the child's illness.

This method allows the loving vibration of the Divine Source to resonate with us, restoring balance and vitality on all levels. Like meditation, creative visualization is of our own manifestation, with no financial burden or invasive procedure. It is through intention on love and awareness of our energy system that we can empower ourselves and our families to heal.

AFFIRMATIONS

An affirmation is a simple, positive statement that asserts something is true. It is a vital exercise in the process of manifesting health and balance in our lives. Human minds continuously run wild with worries, anxieties, and random thoughts. By employing affirmations, we reprogram the mind with statements of positive thoughts, which create and attract everything we desire to manifest in our lives.

The practice of using affirmations is straightforward, with key points to remember for success. It is best to declare your intention in the present tense, as if you have already achieved your goal. The subconscious mind believes what you affirm is the reality and sets the course of action for it to be so. Avoid using negative phrases. Affirmations should be worded in the positive, such as "I feel strong," as opposed to the negative "I don't want to be weak." Make certain your statements are short, specific, and easy to remember. It may help to write them down in your HeartGlow journal or post them on a mirror as a reminder to perform the exercise when you are getting ready in the morning. Take the time to repeat the affirmation and become a believer in the power of creating your own desires.

Similar to meditation and creative visualization, affirmations can be implemented in a multitude of environments, at minimal cost, and put into practice with people of all ages and abilities. Alternative practitioners and allopathic specialists utilize affirmations in supporting those in their care to achieve goals of optimum health and balance in life. Children can be taught this simple technique to not only alter a negative state of mind but also to empower them to heal their physical body from within, an amazing demonstration of the mind-body-spirit connection. Many HeartGlow families now incorporate affirmations as a fun ritual prior to going to bed at night: positive, uplifting statements leading to pleasant dreams and a great start to the next day.

HEARTGLOW EXERCISES

We've discovered how love as a healing practice fosters resonance in the Field of Intuitive Harmony and facilitates deeper individual connections with the Divine energy. We can create a life of love for our children and ourselves! These next two exercises show you how to take small, loving steps toward a life of Divine bliss.

EXERCISE 11: HEARTGLOW AFFIRMATIONS

In this exercise, I would like you to begin by writing five affirmations for yourself in your HeartGlow journal. Keep it simple and begin with areas of life in which you would like to see immediate improvement. Most of us have self-worth issues to work through, so I suggest you include affirmations expressing love and appreciation of self. For example: "I am a beautiful, vibrant person." Your affirmations have to be believable or you will infuse the negative energy of denial into the process. Start with small statements and improve them creatively over time. I find as you fall in love with yourself, your affirmations begin to reflect it.

After you have written your affirmations, make a commitment to yourself to recite them every morning when you get up and each evening before you go to bed. Choose an affirmation for the day and recite it five times at each session. After you have done this for a period of time, add a few of the intuitive parenting affirmations I have written below:

- God has entrusted us with the sacred responsibility of nurturing one another at the soul level.
- My child and I are on a path of Divine Grace and are examples to the world of pure, unconditional love.
- My heart and mind are open to the lessons my child has to teach.
- I celebrate seeing Spirit dance in the eyes of my child and am eager to learn the steps.
- My heart glows from the love and gratitude I have for my life.

Explore affirmations in different ways in your life. A great number of HeartGlow parents enjoy recording their affirmations over and over in their journals or creating an art piece to accompany the statement. You can see how easy it is to integrate affirmations in play with your children. Try these fun activities:

- Recite affirmations at the dinner table with the entire family.
- Break out the crayons and draw a picture to go along with an affirmation.
- Write affirmations on slips of paper and act them out, as in a game of charades.

EXERCISE 12: CELEBRATION OF LOVE

In this exercise, I would like you to dedicate an entire day with your family in celebration of love. Clear everyone's schedules and make your relationships a priority for the entire day by staying at home and doing things together. This is *not* the time to play video games, watch sports, work on the computer, or be on autopilot. You do not need to spend money, take a vacation, or make any significant sacrifice. Simply spend conscious time together. Be present with one another, moment by moment. If a whole day is too much to start with, aim for half a day or a few hours.

Here are some things to do to get you started:

- Play board games, do a puzzle, or paint a "love" picture together.
- Cook a special meal as a family with everyone's favorite recipes.
- Make something together, such as a birdhouse for the yard or decorations for the home.
- Plant flowers, herbs, or even a vegetable garden.
- Sing songs, play music, and have a dance party.
- Go for a walk, ride bikes, or take a family drive to a new place.
- Take the opportunity to do some of your other HeartGlow exercises.

I have fond memories of making paper chains and tissue carnations with my grandmother when I was a young child. We would decorate the entire house with our creations, taking pride in our work. Although it has been over thirty years, I still feel the resonance of those loving moments when I think back to them. Remember, it is the love and pure intention expressed during simple tasks that leave lasting imprints on our hearts.

After your celebration of love, take the time to write about your experiences and impressions in your HeartGlow journal. Did you enjoy the time together? What worked? What didn't? Could you make it the entire day without resorting to watching television or logging on to the computer? If not, write about that too, without judgment. It is difficult to expect immediate closeness and bonding if your family is not in the habit of spending quality time together. Take it bit by bit and work up to longer periods of time. Resonance is not a product of force or struggle. Keep your heart open and attitude light and you'll be on the right track.

SUMMARY OF KEY POINTS

The Divine Essence is the source and expression of all love in the Universe. Learning, demonstrating, and celebrating love within us is the purpose of life itself. This amazing power of love can be clearly represented in the life journey of our families. Each of us has individual relationships, interactions, and experiences that allow for opportunities to let our loving God light to shine.

The choice is ours through our actions and intentions as to whether we live in the expansion of love or in the limitation of fear—deciding for ourselves if we want a life based on freedom and peace, or on control and manipulation. The healing radiance of love flows through all beings yet can be restricted by our inattention to vibration and our lack of knowledge about its process.

Myopic perceptions of love are outside of the Divine Self and do not consider the virtuous universal vibration within us. We need to challenge ourselves to move beyond a limited perspective and expand our definition of love to encompass all. We are each a part of the same Creative Presence of Love—a vibrant inclusive force, not an exclusive club reserved only for those who behave in a certain manner. By raising our children with the conscious awareness of God love energy, we shift our world into a new realm of peace and a time of transcendence for all. We have the opportunity to expand our worlds and experience love without limits. Are you ready to discover the bliss?

The techniques of meditation, creative visualization, and affirmations strengthen love as a healing practice, foster resonance in the Field of Intuitive Harmony, and facilitate deeper individual connections with the Divine. By taking these next steps forward, we empower our society to unleash the healing, loving vibration within us all, creating a life of unlimited possibilities for our children.

Meditation is an exercise of connecting with the Divine Energy through deep relaxation and the absence of active thought. Creative visualization is a technique that utilizes the power of the imagination to manifest balance and healing in life. This practice can be used to address disorders on all levels of existence. An affirmation is a simple, positive statement that asserts something is true. It is a vital exercise in the process of manifesting health and balance in our lives.

HEARTGLOW HINTS FOR INTUITIVE PARENTING

- Raise your vibration with laughter, levity, and exuberance for life.
- Love is expansive. If it has limits or conditions, it is something else.

- Make a list of those you love and why. Feel your energy intensify as you ignite your heart center. Access this sacred place often to restore yourself.
- Know what you love about yourself. Make a pledge to honor yourself every day.
- Send valentines year-round.

PART III

Singing the Song:
Energy in Everyday Life

7

The Sensory
Exploration Approach

*If facts are the seeds that later produce knowledge and wisdom,
then the emotions and the impressions of the senses are the
fertile soil in which the seeds must grow.*

RACHEL CARSON, *THE SENSE OF WONDER*

We are beginning to see the beauty and amazing possibilities available to us through living with an intuitive heart. Parenting our children with the belief and understanding of resonance and energy benefits us in countless ways. To appreciate the excitement of telepathic parenting, we need to put our intention, energy, and effort into overdrive.

A common language of energy must exist between parent and child to be consistent with energy communication. We all get psychic hits—those accurate insights or precognitive visions—yet to rely on this form of expression every day, we need to stay in harmony. Receiving arbitrary symbols or messages that have no mutual understanding only complicates matters. Imagine if your nightly dreams were in Portuguese and you spoke only English. You would be perplexed, frustrated, and even a bit afraid—just as the many who receive psychic signals are but do not speak the language. You can greatly increase the accuracy and comprehension of your energetic correspondence by establishing your own family dialect. We do this through sensory exploration, curbing the ego, and achieving emotional stability.

SENSES OF THE SOUL

Eager for our lives to become less dramatic, we settled back into a comfortable pattern at home following Raegan's emergency road trip to Boston. After almost two years of medical upheaval, it would be a nice change of pace to *just be* for a while. Mark took a new job closer to home and I continued my metaphysical studies while also operating the gift shop. No longer needing to fight for her life, Raegan could use her energy to thrive and discover new pleasures. We were able to swim in the lake, go for walks, and take time to recover from the trauma of it all. Stopping by a small waterfall on our stroll through town, I could see Raegan smile as she listened to the rush of the water. Her vision was often overwhelmed by sunlight, so she spent much of our time outside with her eyes closed tight. The strong scent of pine surrounded us as we rested on a wooden bench for a few moments of peace. The great outdoors gave her plenty to take in with her inquisitive ears and nose. It was a blessing to see Raegan begin to experience the world around her, far from a stark, sterile hospital room.

I wasn't sure our heart communication would continue now that we were no longer knocking at death's door. Did it kick in only for really important stuff? Why did I have it sometimes and not at others? This sacred endowment of mother's intuition was still quite a mystery to me. I could hear my friend Deane's voice echoing in my mind: "What better gift can the Universe give a nonverbal child but a psychic mother?" she said as she placed my astrological natal chart in front of me.

I'd met Deane Driscoll a few years before, at a time when I was looking everywhere for answers to my complicated situation. Bouncing from psychologists to tarot readers to counselors, I yearned to have a complete understanding of what life was all about. Little did I know this psychic astrologer would be the one to have deep insights into the soul connection between my daughter and me. She had specific answers for my countless, probing questions. Over the years, Deane's vast knowledge, compassion, and practical recommendations have provided a sense of cosmic support to my family. She has taught me to believe in the possibilities and to realize the Universe is more beautiful and complex than we can even imagine. Her lessons inspired me to teach parents how they too can communicate with their children with their hearts.

When I made a point of noting when Raegan and I were communicating energetically, I realized it was happening frequently—and in more ways than I had first thought. Yes, there were the obvious moments when Raegan's own voice came into my head, yet there were also more subtle times when I just sensed things from her. In fact, all of my physical senses seemed to be enhanced now to appreciate the subtle energies. Of course! That is why things seemed to glow when I looked at them. Certain phrases and sounds stood out when I heard them. The sound of my own voice conveyed my intentions even more than the words I formed. Messages didn't just come as pictures in the mind's eye or as an internal voice; the sixth sense was actually a conductor from the soul that used my entire being as an instrument. Every part of us naturally processes energy—our hearts, minds, and senses all work together.

Enjoying simple activities with my daughter added to our energy repertoire. We were learning about all of this together. Our shared experience gave us a common vocabulary to choose from.

One late spring morning, Raegan and I stretched out on a blanket on the lawn feeling the grass and dirt with our curious fingers. The various scents in the yard were distinctive and enjoyable to us both. Later in evening as I tucked her snuggly into bed, chatting away about our day, the smell of moist soil permeated the room. "Yes, the dirt did smell wonderful, didn't it?" I said as I kissed her good-night. I laughed to myself, thinking Raegan could now send me scent-o-grams. She was continuing to do whatever she could to reach out to us.

There were many frustrating times when I wasn't able to sense anything from Raegan. It was infuriating to be communicating openly one day and then feeling as though my transmitter and receiver had broken down the next. Crying and yelling at myself, I would lumber through the house, sulking. The worse I felt, the more static disrupted the channel. What was the common denominator in these situations? Me. Specifically, I was too wrapped up in my own dramas and over-identifying with the ego aspect of myself. As doubt, fear, and frustration crept in, the noise within became too loud for me to appreciate the more subtle energy communication. I needed to be mindful of what chatter I allowed on the line. This is why most of us don't hear the messages from our higher selves; we are too busy humoring our personalities and ego to truly listen.

ENERGY, EMOTION, AND EGO

It is a common misunderstanding and oversimplification that emotions are the sole means of energy communication. I understand the theory behind Spirit "speaking" through our emotions, yet I believe energy communication encompasses all levels of causation—physical, mental, emotional, and spiritual. We would do ourselves a great disservice by seeing it only from an emotional perspective. In my experience, I am most connected when clear, balanced, and in a place slightly beyond emotion.

Emotion is a state of being most associated with the mind and personality, not necessarily with workings of the higher self. Although emotion can be a powerful motivator and conveyor of intention, we need to remember we humans are often fickle creatures and can contradict ourselves with the vast swaying emotions of our fragile egos. Look back to an experience when you were extremely upset or emotionally frantic, and you can see why it was not the best time to make a decision or interpret the meaning of communication. I've had a great number of misunderstandings with people over the years when I allowed my poor mood to dictate my perception of an event. Haven't you?

Many people mistakenly believe we need to react to our feelings in the moment. For example, if anger surfaces in you, then you need to judge the situation as bad energy that should be confronted or avoided. This is not necessarily so, as the judgments, addictions, and projections from our egos jade our perceptions, leaving us without the ability to sense details clearly. Our feelings and emotions can shift with the wind and are easily triggered by fear. I encourage you to feel your emotions and then move through them without clinging on or defining yourself by them. To accurately evaluate our energetic environment, we need to be in a state of clarity and balance, allowing our subtle energy system to do its job. Taking time to quiet the mind and our emotional state allows us to hear the inner whispers of our soul.

Ancient mystics advised a heightened level of detachment to avoid the pitfall of emotional and thought-choked turbulence. A valuable technique, yet I find detachment difficult to accomplish where our children are concerned. Instead of thinking of it as *detachment*, let's call it *spiritual attachment*—loving our children at the highest levels possible. We can experience the levels beyond personality and ego. It is essential we develop the skills to bypass our ego's habits by turning to spiritual love as the ultimate filter. Step outside yourself to a higher perspective. Look lovingly at the big picture of the Universe. We are each vibrant souls, equal in every way and a part of a greater whole.

A common challenge parents face on their intuitive parenting journeys is projecting their desires onto a situation—basically, wanting something to be other than what it is. When we force our wills in a particular circumstance, we are depriving ourselves and our children of actually communicating with one another. We cannot hear them over ourselves. If our egos are in the way, we cannot be sure if what we are sensing is true energy communication. It may be merely what we want to hear. I realized Raegan was communicating with me because her information and message was outside of my own will and field of experience. I was only able to hear her when I stepped away from my own desires and projections of the situation at hand.

One father of a nonverbal child believed his son loved the New York Yankees as much as he did, although the son's energy said otherwise to his mom and me—that he was a Red Sox fan. Regardless of what we detected in our contacts with the child, the father held strongly to his belief his son was just like him. Finally, the father tested our suggestion by gifting his son with a Red Sox hat. The child's smile said it all. Until the father was able to get out from under his own projections, he could not appreciate the truth of the situation and the fun rivalry between their teams. He needed to get over himself to feel the true bliss of their energetic bond.

You can see by this example how easy it would be to diminish the likelihood of actual communication by simply wanting a certain result and projecting it forward as the truth. I find this happens with families all the time, even during traditional verbal dialogue. We only need to be acutely mindful of our ego and intentions to get past this hurdle. Remember, if you choose to project one absolute reality, you are closing the door to all other possibilities. The ecstasy you feel when you have heard from your child energetically is better than you could ever dream, yet to hear them you need to listen.

LISTENING WITH OUR BODIES

Listening is such a simple act. It requires us to be present,
and that takes practice, but we don't have to do anything else.
We don't have to advise, or coach, or sound wise.
We just have to be willing to sit there and listen.
—MARGARET J. WHEATLEY, "LISTENING IS HEALING"

To put the Sensory Exploration Approach into action, we need to commit to using our senses in a heightened state of awareness. Perceive with every part of our being as an instrument of Spirit. We hold ourselves back by not loving, living, and working to our full potential. This is one of the most valuable lessons Raegan has taught me. As limited as she is in so many ways, she uses everything at her disposal in celebration of her existence. Imagine what our world would be like if we all did the same.

This sensory method develops an energy language within your own family and can be implemented regardless of your child's age or ability level. By sharing experiences and maintaining sharp awareness, we create an energy repertoire unique to our own Field of Intuitive Harmony. For example, think back to the sight, smell, and taste of your grandmother's apple pie on Thanksgiving. The mere thought of it triggers feelings, sensations, and memories for you and other family members. Your grandmother baked the intention of love into the pie. Close your eyes and open yourself to the energy of your grandmother's love; you can still feel it even if she has long since passed away. We must remember: energy is eternal and *always* exists. It cannot be created or destroyed; energy merely changes form.

By experiencing the world around us with heightened perception, we allow the magnificent flow of energy into our lives. Action supports our intentions, thus strengthening our common bond, increasing the likelihood of successful energy communication. When doing these activities together, please use all five of your physical senses: touch, taste, hearing, sight, and smell. Think of your sixth sense as the internal glow of clarity wrapped around each of our other senses.

In addition to following the ten suggestions listed below, several HeartGlow families have constructed sensory boxes to use on an ongoing basis, which can be especially helpful with young or special-needs children. This is easily accomplished by filling containers with items from around the house, such as dried beans, coffee, fabrics, cotton balls, and so on. There really is no limit to all you can do. The most important point is to be aware during the activity— truly take it all in. I am sure you will discover a few things about your own energy and emotions along the way. Beyond these specific suggestions, challenge yourself to increase your sensory awareness in everything you do. Be mindful of what you are processing as you experience the world. Take yourself off autopilot and begin to honor the vibrancy of life—our greatest gift from God.

Sensory Exploration Activities You Can Do with Your Family

1. **Go for a walk.** Whether in the woods or on a city street, the outside world is filled with many incredible experiences for our senses to dive into. Take your family for a stroll

out and about to discover the tantalizing things just outside your door.

2. **Visit an animal farm.** By going to a farm or petting zoo, you and your child will be able to appreciate the vast sensory life of animals and their caretakers. Be sure to help clean stalls and feed and brush the animals.

3. **Take a trip to the ocean.** Life at the seaside is unlike any other place on Earth. With its own unique smells, textures, and sensations, the beach offers unlimited experiences. Take a swim, splash in the waves, make a sandcastle, or discover the tiny life in a tidal pool.

4. **Work in the garden.** Dirt, weeds, flowers, and worms— just a small sample of all there is to discover by tending a garden. Whether you have one in your yard or volunteer at a farm or community center, gardening as a family is fun, healthy, and educational.

5. **Explore the contents of the kitchen.** Sort through your food, utensils, and canisters, exploring the sights, smells, sounds, and tastes of what you find. This is a great way to clean out the fridge, drawers, and cabinets. Raegan loves to feel dried beans and rice with her fingers.

6. **Bake a pie, cake, or batch of cookies.** Delicious and fun. Make a family dessert together, learning how the wet and dry ingredients combine for a tasty treat. How do things taste individually? Then mixed together? Remember, the love and fun memories you are creating will be triggered any time you smell warm cookies in the future.

7. **Visit your elders.** There is no better experience for learning than spending time with our elderly loved ones. Appreciating the struggles and triumphs of their daily lives can give us great insight to the mysteries of our own. Valuing and sharing this time with our children is our blessing and responsibility. Spend time with your own relatives and also volunteer at your local nursing home.

8. **Play dress up.** Take a journey of sight, sound, and texture by wearing fun clothes and costumes. Tell the stories associated with the fancy dresses and old coats from your past. Allow the beads, scarves, and jewelry to transport you and your child to the realm of fun and fantasy.

9. **Clean out your attic or storage room.** What may seem like a chore to you can be a fun activity for your child. Hidden treasures, old family photos, and high school trophies are just the ingredients for delicious discovery.

10. **Lie in the grass and ponder the stars.** This simple act of being peaceful under the night sky can foster clarity, balance, and love in numerous aspects of your life. Do you remember when you first heard the crickets and felt the whisper of the evening air? Your child will too.

Notice none of these activities involve sitting in front of the television or computer, or incorporate any artificial stimuli. In this method, we are striving for natural experiences to nurture our senses on all levels of existence, thus deepening our understanding of the world around us. There is a place in life for multimedia; however, it should not take the place of our own direct experience. Like so many other things, we need to find the proper balance. Why sit slouched on the couch watching strangers on television living life to the fullest? Get out there and do some living for yourself.

I am a firm believer that much of what we need to rouse our senses exists in our own natural environment. You do not need to purchase products or invest in equipment that simulates sound, scent, or taste. If you use essential oils for aromatherapy, go for organic varieties. Our bodies know how to process what is natural, so aim for things in their pure form and not chemicals trying to be real. A good example of this is fruit-flavored gum and candy. They often smell strong and taste sweet but rarely capture the true essence of whatever fruit they are mimicking. Going for a walk in a berry patch pleases the taste buds and the soul.

Several years ago, while taking a class on Spirit communication under the direction of world-renowned psychic medium James Van Praagh, I learned the significance of deep sensory knowledge. Many of us mediums in training would get information through a taste in our mouths or by detecting an aroma in the air. The energy of the departed person was using the known physical senses of the medium/channel to get their point across. It was more than a whispered sound or a mind's eye vision. Our sense of taste and smell allowed yet another avenue for the energy to take. It is extremely compelling and profoundly moving to witness energy communication at this level. Mr. Van Praagh has dedicated his life to delivering messages from Spirit and educating the masses on the power and magnificence of eternal energy. I am immensely grateful for all he has given the world and specifically for the encouragement he has given me and other parents of nonverbal children.

This is an opportunity to charge your Field of Intuitive Harmony with powerful images, events, and information to draw upon. Think of sensory exploration as instilling and initiating your own energy and experience language. Our senses take in so much more than we can intellectually appreciate. By intensely focusing our physical senses, we actually increase our ability to be aware in the world, leading to development of energy appreciation and a heightened sixth sense. We have become accustomed to zooming through life with little attention to the magnificent details around us. We must take the time to slow down and experience the full flavor and richness of our lives by sampling from the menu of life and satisfying our sensory appetites.

HEARTGLOW EXERCISES

Throughout this chapter we have learned how our five physical senses are crucial to understanding our soul sense, or sixth sense. These senses work together to give us heightened clarity in our daily experience. The next two exercises get you started on sensory exploration, a valuable item in your intuitive parenting toolbox.

EXERCISE 13: BE YOUR CHILD

In this HeartGlow exercise, I would like you to see the world as your child does. By putting ourselves in the shoes of another, we develop a greater understanding of their perspective on life. By appreciating their unique position and energy signature, we can better relate to our children and resonate within the Field of Intuitive Harmony. So kick off your heels or work boots and slide into your child's sneakers. It's time to use all of your senses—to be your child.

This exercise is best done when you have the house to yourself, so you do not have to explain to your kids why you are exploring their space so closely. It's important to note here: you are not to snoop or invade the privacy of your child by going through their things. Trust goes both ways. Your focus should be exploring the energy of their primary surroundings from their perspective. To do this, set the proper intention by beginning with the HeartGlow Primer. When you are in a comfortable, relaxed state, you may begin.

Go to your child's room and lie down on the bed. Closing your eyes, ask Spirit and your child's higher self for permission to look into his/her energetic space. This is a journey of love that will allow you greater understanding of your child's daily existence and soul's path. Express your genuine desire to be open, kind, and peaceful. You are merely asking for an opportunity to connect with him/her at a higher level. When you feel ready, slowly open your eyes to begin the next stage of the exercise.

Staying in your child's room or primary living space, begin to take in the environment as you feel your child would. Literally, pretend to be your child. How would he/she feel? What does your child like there? Experience it through each of your five physical senses. What do you see? Hear? Smell? Taste? Touch? Utilizing all these senses, can you detect patterns that you may not have noticed before? Soft things? Hard things? Certain colors, shapes, or smells?

If your child has a particular disability or physical limitation, please try to re-create it the best you can. For example, wear a blindfold if your child has no sight. What does that do to your sense of hearing? My daughter is often on a play mat on the floor, so is horizontal most of the time, looking to the ceiling. She has never experienced the world from a standing position. I discovered the beauty of the fan and patterns on the ceiling when I looked from Raegan's perspective. I also discovered what she could not see, which I had previously assumed she could.

After you explore the environment with each of your physical senses, intentionally utilize your soul sense and intuitive heart. Do you have to close your eyes to see with your mind's eye? It is very common to have to do this at first, as you limit one sense to heighten the other. In time, you will no longer need to do this, as you'll have practice and greater skill with your subtle senses. Be in your child's shoes for a moment. Get a sense of his/her feelings, thoughts, and dreams. Can you sense how your child's aura feels or looks?

Investigate his/her life energetically for as long as you feel comfortable. As you near the end of the exercise, express gratitude to your child and your own higher self for participating in the activity. With the experience fresh in your mind, write your reflections in your HeartGlow journal. Make sure to note if you learned anything specific or even received a message from your child or Spirit. Heart-Glow families have disclosed significant results with this particular exercise, such as realizing their child needed eyeglasses or being able to appreciate the severity of a child's phobia. This is a valuable intuitive parenting method available to you now to gain greater insight into the life and energy experience of your child.

EXERCISE 14: SENSORY OVERLOAD

Many HeartGlow families are concerned that their children are often irritable and combative due to overstimulation, or seem to get easily upset in crowds and public places. Their sweet, engaging children become like grumpy strangers when in the mall or even at a large family gathering. It is essential for parents to realize all children deal with stimuli in different ways and can be overwhelmed due to their energetic sensitivities. We, as adults, forget what it is like to be a sponge soaking it all in, as we have developed dense buffers and are not as energetically acute as our children.

Intuitive professionals often compare children's energy overload to having every noisy appliance in your home running at the same time. Think what it would be like to have a number of televisions or radios on simultaneously, all tuned to a different program and at full volume. This would make it difficult to think, hear, speak, and see clearly. A child with heightened energy sensitivity can get this feeling from a normal environment, as all the people around them are energy transmitters and receivers.

In this HeartGlow exercise, I would like you to experience a complete sensory overload. Go to a room in your home where you have access to multiple lights and appliances. This could be your living room, kitchen, bedroom, or office. One by one, begin to turn things on. Start with the lights, making sure each overhead fixture, lamp, and sconce is on. Now turn on the radio to a comfortable volume and to a station you like. Now do the same with the television, ensuring the volume is also on and at a normal level you listen to. One by one, turn on any remaining appliances. Children's toys? Electric toothbrush? Hair dryer? CD player? Make sure your windows are letting in light, wind, sounds, and smells from the street.

You get the idea: complete chaos. In this state, we are distracted from our own internal sense of being because of the external pollution. Our heart rate and anxiety level are increased. Our breathing is more labored. Stress levels begin to wreak havoc within our bodies. It would be difficult to speak or do a basic math equation, let alone trying to center oneself or say a prayer. This frustrating and overwhelming feeling is akin to being in acute energy overload.

Now, one by one, slowly turn off each appliance and appreciate the change within yourself as things begin to regulate. Do you feel calmer? What thoughts begin to run through your mind? How does your body feel? As you continue to ease away from the chaos and into serenity, make note of how you feel physically, mentally, and emotionally. Just imagine the levels of peace you have yet to discover as you explore the inner corridors of your soul.

Many of the exercises throughout this book help us balance the subtle energy systems of our families and facing energy overload. Although each child and situation is unique, I find it helpful to use the Aura Wash technique on a daily basis as well as teaching our children to honestly express their discomfort, so the situation at hand can be addressed. For example, if they get a stomachache while shopping, you can address it with one of the intuitive parenting tools you have learned here. You will begin to recognize the particular triggers your child has and can use your own intuition to address them. For some children it is the roar of a crowd, for others the tone and temper of a particular family member that sets them off. Intuitive parenting allows us to understand our children are reacting to energy discordance, which we now have the skills to address.

SUMMARY OF KEY POINTS

Parenting our children with the belief and understanding of resonance and energy benefits us in countless ways. To appreciate the excitement of telepathic parenting, we need to put our intention, energy, and effort into overdrive. A common language of energy must exist between parent and child to be truly consistent with energy communication. You can greatly increase the accuracy and comprehension of your energetic correspondence by establishing your own family dialect. We do this through sensory exploration and establishing emotional clarity.

The judgments and projections from our egos often jade our perceptions, leaving us without the ability to see clearly. To accurately access our energetic environment, we need to be in a state of clarity and balance. We must develop the skills to bypass our ego's habits by turning to spiritual love as the ultimate filter. We are each vibrant souls on a journey, equal in every way and a part of a greater whole. If our egos are in the way, we cannot be sure that what we are sensing is true energy communication and not just what *we want to hear*. If you choose to project only one absolute reality, you are closing the door to all other possibilities.

To put the Sensory Exploration Approach into action, we need to commit to using our senses in a heightened state of awareness. Perceive with every part of our being. We hold ourselves back by not loving, living, and working to our full potential. This method develops an energy language within your own family and can be implemented regardless of your child's age or ability level. Through sharing common experiences with sharp awareness, we create an energy repertoire unique to our own Field of Intuitive Harmony.

Action supports our intentions, thus strengthening our common bond, increasing the likelihood of successful energy communication. When doing these activities together, please use all five of your physical senses: touch, taste, hearing, sight, and smell. Think of your sixth sense as the internal glow of clarity wrapped around each of our other senses. By intensely focusing with our physical senses, we actually increase our ability to be aware in the world, leading to development of energy appreciation and a heightened sixth sense.

HeartGlow Hints for Intuitive Parenting

- Investigate your environment for your family's sensory triggers.
- Put your nose to the test on a walk about town to heighten your sense of smell. Scent is a great addition to your intuitive toolbox.
- Create a quiet chamber, devoid of light, sound, and other stimuli. Spend time inside and journal your experience.
- Awaken your textural sensitivity by touching things as a child would.
- Add a new colorful, eclectic food to your diet each week. Discover a fruit or vegetable from another part of the world and share it with your family.

8

Self-Healing for Parents

I love people. I love my family, my children ... but inside myself
is a place where I live all alone and that's where you
renew your springs that never dry up.

PEARL S. BUCK

Discovering the bliss of intuitive parenting comes more easily
to those who have health, truth, and balance in their world.
When our lives are in order, we are able to see beyond the chaos,
make clear decisions, and confidently face any challenge that
comes our way. Maintaining a dedicated perspective on well-being
enables you as a parent to fully support and nurture your children:
mind, body, and spirit. To foster peace and wellness for your family,
you must demonstrate and emanate your own best intentions. It is
time for you to stand up and be the healthy model. Your loving
advice to not smoke, for example, is ludicrous if you have a two-
pack-a-day habit. Actions do speak louder than words and should
be in alignment with your intent. Energy speaks even louder, making
any contradiction between intention and behavior obvious. Living
a conscious life, mindful and focused, allows your Divine light to
brilliantly shine and be the best example for your child. Together,
you can do anything!

THE MOSAIC OF ME

I would like to say my balance with the Universe came early in this journey, as if I was bestowed with grand cosmic wisdom a week or so after Raegan's birth. Nothing could be further from the truth. Although I feel I now have a greater perspective on my existence and how things have evolved in my world, those first few years of motherhood posed challenges with depression, low self-esteem, and my physical health.

My depression was tricky and unpredictable to manage. It was not day after day of heart-wrenching despair, as there were many good days peppered in with the difficult ones—times when I felt hopeful and optimistic, believing my child would be the exception to every rule and would defy all negative expectations assigned by the medical community. I ignored the chronic stress I was under and suppressed the emotional pain, which lurked deep within. Most people would never have guessed I was enormously depressed, as I had a positive word or hopeful smile when they would ask how we were doing. In those first few years, I became an expert at hiding my true state of being, even from my husband, mother, and close friends. No one knew angry trees were growing up around me, blocking the warmth and light of the sun.

Mark and I were starting to drive each other crazy. Our moods often collided, and we spent much of our time together avoiding intimate conversation. We talked at length about medical issues, bills, and day-to-day occurrences, but we rarely connected with one another. Our roles of Mom and Dad were consuming every part of us, leaving nothing for our relationship or our own personal pursuits. Not putting positive energy into our connection, we actually fed the negativity by sniping at each other about superficial and ridiculous things.

Like me, Mark was overwhelmed, fearful, and frustrated. He began complaining about crumbs on the countertop, piles of laundry in the bedroom, and his hard day at work. Truthfully, at the time, I didn't care. Not even noticing what the house looked like, I would roll my eyes after he left the room and resent his comments. Household concerns seemed minor to me now. I was trying to survive motherhood and comprehend the deep mysteries of the Universe. Somehow dusting and window washing had lost their allure.

AngelBaby was growing fast. Her big blue eyes and joyful smile gave me encouragement as we went about our day. If she could face her challenges with such a courageous spirit, I could certainly try. Raegan kept me focused on living in the moment, each one bringing new lessons on inner strength and my heart's capacity to love. At times I felt strong enough to carry the world on my shoulders, yet at others I felt weak, wanting to curl up in a ball and cry.

A few of my friends also had young children and would come over to visit while our spouses were at work. The scene was not far from the ideal days of playing house as young girls in the backyard—except my daughter was disabled. That's something you never consider when you are eight, dangling your plastic baby doll by the arm while eating an orange Popsicle. It was nice to share my home and my daughter with friends, Popsicles or not.

My friend's son, Gavin, was born just a week after Raegan. Carrie and I enjoyed our mutual pregnancies by taking silly belly pictures together and indulging our food cravings. It was so fun to go through it as a team, beaming with happiness and planning the next eighteen years with our children as playmates. Now our reality was different. We struggled with the issues of sadness, guilt, and joy all being jumbled up together. Having our children in the same room was a constant reminder of what wouldn't be for Raegan, the milestones she would never even come near.

I had tried to tune out traditional milestones right after Raegan's birth and didn't look to compare her with any other child. It was hard with Gavin, though, as they were so close in age. Carrie and I weren't comfortable talking freely about our children's accomplishments, as we didn't want to upset each other. Besides, how could I expect anyone to understand the small victories we celebrated? It would be like comparing apples to artichokes.

During one of their visits, Gavin said, "Momma . . . Momma," showing her a toy car in his hand. It was the first time I'd heard him speak. Tears welling in my eyes, I didn't know if I was proud of him or sad for me. Carrie and I started crying with our small children eyeing us cautiously. Raegan let out a squeal and a laugh as Gavin zoomed by her with his car. "Boy, do we have to get past this," I said. "They are fine with it, so we should be too." We hugged each other tight, vowing to talk through our feelings whenever we needed to. Both of our children, beautiful beings of light, were exactly as God intended.

It started to occur to me, if Raegan was exactly as God had intended, maybe I was also as the Universe intended. Are we all priceless works of art and just don't know it? Sitting in meditation on the floor of my bedroom, colorful pictures of my lifetime flashed before me. From my celestial perch, I was able to see for the first time how every experience, each moment I lived, had brought me to where I now sat. I began to understand how certain events provided knowledge I now needed. Each relationship, job, trip, every psychic experience—all had a miraculous connection to the present moment. Nothing was out of place or by accident. It all fit perfectly with no rights, wrongs, or regrets. The life images curiously floated before my eyes, unveiling the intricate mosaic of me.

Although my spiritual world was beginning to blossom during this time, my physical health suffered significantly during Raegan's early years due to lack of nurturing. I wasn't making *me* a priority, so I gained weight from eating junk food, relaxing at night with a bottle of wine, and not getting enough exercise. I was in and out of the doctor's office for headaches, allergies, stress, viruses, and a number of other ailments. My physical body was dramatically out of balance, neglected, and beginning to wear the scars of my emotional and mental wounds. Cupcakes and Merlot may be comforting in the moment, but they didn't satisfy what I was truly hungry for: a succulent slice of inner peace.

Pain and frustration would be there for me to cling to as long as I wanted that life. It was a choice for me to make. Did I want a life of victimization or empowerment? The trek in the dark forest was my chosen path, until I was ready to change direction and emerge into the clearing on my own. Reaching a point where I was tired of being sick and depressed, I knew change was needed. It was time to take the theories I was studying out of the books and put them into practice—time to walk the walk of well-being, love myself, and live an energetic life.

The decision to make conscious changes in the way I lived led to powerful transformations. Beginning to love myself, I could finally see the value in caring for my whole being, and this greatly benefited my family. What was good for me was also good for them. Physically, I began to eat better, take long walks, and stretch my fatigued muscles. I opened up to discover who I was as an emotional being, working through issues that greatly affected my marriage: abandonment, anger, and self-worth. I stretched my mental abilities by taking courses, writing, and teaching. My spiritual interests grew as I pursued ancient philosophies, meditation, and gatherings of like-minded people.

These changes allowed me to see the light of God shining vibrantly in everyone and everything. I perceived each being as more than any role we played. Although we were parents, wives, husbands, daughters, and sons, we were also fragments of the

Divine on our own individual sojourns on Earth. I now understood we are free to make choices about how we live, love, and evolve. Our choices create our reality. No one needs to remain a victim of circumstance, a puppet to anyone's projections, or the controller of another's will. We have the freedom to exist in whatever manner we desire according to our personal values, beliefs, and goals. I realized I could create a life of love and happiness, a life of sheer bliss, by merely choosing to do so.

Letting Go

To put the world right in order, we must first put the nation
in order; to put the nation in order, we must first put the
family in order; to put the family in order, we must first
cultivate our personal life; we must first set our hearts right.
—Confucius

Self-healing begins with the firm belief that you are the creator of your own life and have the ability to manifest lasting change in your world. We become the best parents we can be by first taking care of ourselves and being vibrant examples to our children of the benefits of self-care. Knowing the responsibility lies only with you is liberating, and also intimidating. It is so much easier to blame circumstances, situations, and people outside of us for our present state of being. However, truth be told, your life is up to you. The mysteries of the Universe are unfolding right before our eyes in amazing, magical ways. We need to wake up from the daze of a mindless existence to take an active role in creating a beautiful life for our families and ourselves. Empowering your children with a deep sense of self-worth will benefit them in all the stages of their lives.

Moving forward with a healthy, balanced perspective requires you to release your attachments to the past and the future. You cannot live in the now by clinging tightly to experiences gone by or dictating every moment to come. Allow yourself to let go of the baggage of unrealized expectations, toxic relationships, labels, and societal projections. If this is difficult to even consider, you need to recognize *you are more than the story you tell*. You are more than a parent, more than an underpaid worker, more than a victim of a crime, betrayal, or injustice.

Everyone faces challenges along the way. The daily responsibilities and burdens that confront all families can be considerable and are often magnified when they're also living with a chronic illness, addiction, or disability of a family member. Although we have all felt alone, misunderstood, and overwhelmed by life's journey, we must remember we are one with the All, brilliantly interconnected by the intuitive energy of our hearts. Every experience contributes color and texture to our life mosaic and need not dictate all of who we are.

Being mindful and proactive in all aspects of life is the clear path to wellness. Knowing our state of health physically, mentally, emotionally, and spiritually allows us to take the responsibility in our own hands and create a life of peace, balance, and clarity. This greater sense of self opens the door to an incredible world of energetic possibilities. Experiencing less pain, increased vitality, and reduced stress enables us to be the best intuitive parents we can be. By opening your heart to wellness, you foster an entirely new way of being.

PHYSICAL WELLNESS

Physical health begins with having a great respect for our body and its complicated systems and functions. Many of us have forgone the care of our bodies by eating unconsciously, ignoring our body's signals, and not being physically active. Physical wellness requires us to be mindful of how we eat, drink, sleep, and exercise.

Our children learn so much from our own behavior, so be the healthy model for your family. If you are looking for an opportunity to increase your intuitive abilities, begin with the vehicle that holds your soul—your amazingly beautiful body. Take the time to visit your physician to develop a healthy protocol that would best suit you. Here are activities and behaviors I recommend for getting you started on a path to physical wellness:

- Eat whole, natural foods, such as fresh fruits, fresh vegetables, and lean proteins. Avoid foods laden with chemical additives, artificial sweeteners, and preservatives. If you choose to indulge on desserts, alcohol, and simple carbohydrates, keep your intake to a minimum. A balanced diet is best for the entire family.
- Maintain a healthy form by being active every day. Take a walk together, dance to ecstatic music, or paddle a kayak. Keep your fitness schedule fun by being diverse and creative. You need not be a professional athlete to appreciate the benefits of a strong body. Regardless of your age, ability, or size, you can develop a program appropriate for you and your family.
- Getting proper rest is a challenge for any parent, especially when our children are young or require special attention. It is essential we find down time for our entire being to rejuvenate. Reduce caffeine intake, avoid stressful activities, and add a brief meditation prior to bed to ease into a more relaxed, centered state. Teaching our children the benefits of tranquility early on helps them establish positive lifelong behaviors.

MENTAL WELLNESS

After long days at work or with the kids, it is easy to zone out in front of the television and collapse. We often feel overworked, yet underutilized. Life can become frustrating when we sense we are merely going through the motions and not being intellectually stimulated. It is important to be involved in thought-provoking activities. We need to make the choice to stay sharp. "Use it or lose it," as they say. Challenging ourselves mentally keeps us young, vibrant, and smart. The increased confidence you garner carries over effortlessly into your intuitive pursuits. Try a few of these techniques to keep your mental gears turning:

- Sign up for a class at your local college, technical school, or community center. Dedicating time to intellectual interests can revitalize your sense of self and give needed respite from family obligations. You will learn new skills, meet interesting people, and rediscover parts of yourself long ago abandoned.
- Organize a book club, poetry circle, or hobby group for your friends. Getting together with those we care about can be a positive, uplifting experience. Add stimulating conversation to the mix to discover your friends' intellectual interests. It can be illuminating and rewarding.
- Expand your comfort zone by learning a new language, instrument, or art form—basket weaving, jewelry making, or writing short stories in your journal. Creative pursuits not only stimulate the mind but also enhance intuitive abilities.

EMOTIONAL WELLNESS

Emotional well-being and a positive sense of self are crucial components to living a happy life and fundamental to successful intuitive parenting. When emotions are in balance, we are able to perceive the world with heightened awareness and feel confident following our energetic insights. If we are out of balance, our insecurities stand in the way of accurate communication and can negatively shape our families. We owe it to ourselves and our loved ones to work through our issues, detach from ego's stranglehold, and live a positive life. Keep these suggestions in mind while on the path to emotional peace:

- Get the support you need by seeking out a counselor, therapist, or close friend to talk to. There are now numerous professionals who incorporate energy techniques with traditional therapy. It is essential to deal with your emotions. If you bury them deep inside they tend to surface later as illness, resentment, or fear.
- Learn to forgive yourself and others. Do not allow a deep sense of guilt or anger from the past to rob you of the present moment and negatively color your future. Releasing ourselves from the projections of others and allowing others to be free from our projections are liberating and life-altering behaviors. Simply choose to let go.
- Take time alone to release pent up emotions. Whether you scream at the ocean, punch pillows, have a good cry, or work out at the gym, find a safe outlet to discharge the energy of negative emotion. You'll be surprised how wonderful it feels to get it all out.

SPIRITUAL WELLNESS

Spiritual well-being provides us a sense of belonging and connectedness in the face of life's varied experiences. Knowing we are part of something greater than our own individual personality and physical being allows us to appreciate the magnificence of the Universe. Regardless of the path or belief system we choose for ourselves, we are blessed souls, free to worship as we please. Feeling the inner glow of Divine love is a comfort in any storm, the light that leads the way in dark places. Open your heart to spiritual expression by exploring these activities:

- Find your place of fellowship. Join a church, synagogue, mosque, Bible study group, or other place of community worship. Surrounding ourselves with others living a life of faith allows us to feel supported in our decision to make Spirit a priority. There is no wrong path to tread. You need only determine which path resonates with you.
- Take a yoga class to discover the inner peace that stems from the meditation, poses, and beliefs associated with this form. It is more than stretching for physical fitness! Yoga is beneficial to our mind, body, emotions, and spirit. Allow its inner calm to wash over you as a wave glides over the sand.
- Contemplate your being. Determine for yourself who you are and what you believe yourself to be in this vast expanse of Universe. Find your inner philosopher by asking the big questions of yourself and patiently awaiting the answers that come from deep within. Be with nature. Read. Meditate. Pray. Take the time to explore your spiritual self.

ENERGETIC WELLNESS

We are vibrant beings of energy, continually sending and receiving signals with our intuitive hearts. Throughout this book, we learn how crucial our subtle energy system is to our daily lives and how we need to be proactive in maintaining balance and clarity. We can champion energetic wellness to our families by demonstrating a healthy respect for this complex system and living with a glowing heart. You can assist your family energetically only if you are harmonious, clear, and open to the Divine flow. Be mindful of these techniques as you integrate energy into your life:

- Start and end each day with a clearing exercise. Quickly visualize your aura and clean up any debris in your biofield. Blast away any toxic energy with the wash of vibrant colors and the intention of love and peace. You are the caretaker of your own energy field, so you are responsible for what you are carrying around.
- Dedicate a minimum of ten minutes each day for energetic communication with your highest self. This is the time to ask your questions about day-to-day events and await the answers. How should you move forward with this or that? Just ask. Journal your explorations to track your progress.
- Stretch your intuitive muscles by playing psychic games. This builds confidence and helps determine how *your* subtle energy system communicates. You can start with who may be on the phone or the color of the tie your boss will wear tomorrow, and then make up tasks of your own. This is not a competition and should be done with a playful spirit. Your accuracy just may surprise you!

HeartGlow Exercises

We are all works of art created by the Universe as a unique expression of itself, a fragment of the Divine source. Appreciating your own significance in this world enables you to live a life of peace and love. You cannot truly care for and nurture the spirit of another until you first cherish the self. The next two exercises assist you in delving into the depths of you.

Exercise 15: A Meditative Mosaic

This exercise is an opportunity for you to relax and connect with yourself at higher levels in contemplation of your life and soul's journey. Who are you? Where have you been in this life? Where are you going next? What has brought you to the place you now sit? It is a time to put worries and family concerns aside to ponder the beautiful mosaic of you, an opportunity to appreciate your every hue, intricate facet, angle, and side—all of what makes you a priceless work of art.

To prepare for this exercise, dress in comfortable clothing and find a space in your home where you can meditate in privacy. You may play instrumental music or nature sounds in the background if you feel it will help you to relax. If you wish to follow these instructions word for word, read them into a recorder to be played at the time of your meditation. I recommend you sit upright on the floor, in a chair, or using a meditation cushion. Lying down risks dozing off, so please try to remain in a seated position with your back straight. Begin with the HeartGlow Primer to get yourself in a balanced and relaxed state.

Slowly take a long, deep breath through your nose and then gently exhale out your mouth. Repeat this three times, permitting your body to ease into the exercise by relaxing all tense muscles. Close your eyes slightly and bring your attention inward. Allow the random thoughts that come to you to float away without drawing your focus. There is no room for worry here. We are entering a realm of pure love and self-acceptance. In your mind, begin to count down from ten to one, knowing you will be at peace when you have reached the final number. Keep your breath slow and steady, letting the calm wash over you. This is your time—an opportunity to connect with Source.

Now that you are comfortable and relaxed, ask Spirit to show you the miraculous images of your life's journey. Remaining detached from emotion, merely perceive the images as they come to you. What do you see? A home you used to live in? A rose garden you wandered by? A toy? Maybe you see an old friend from school, a beloved pet or teacher from long ago. Who has crossed your path and left imprints on your heart? See the places, events, and people that have contributed to your experiences. These impressions need not be good or bad, they just are. Allow the faces, names, pictures, and symbols to flow freely without resistance on your part. Take yourself far back, looking for pictures from your infancy and early childhood. Feel the resonance of those you encounter, even if they have long ago departed from earth.

Utilizing all your intuitive senses, is there anything you hear, smell, or feel? Is that a squeaky door you hear or a splash of water on your face? Could it be the smell of the ocean or Grandma's favorite recipe stewing on the stove? What are you experiencing now? Where is your soul taking you? Explore the years of your life through images, sounds, aromas, and sensations. See the beauty you are in the mosaic before you. Perceive the vibrant smile of your child, which mirrors your own. Appreciate the flirtatious wink of an old love, stirring energy from your heart center. Feel the slap on your face from a betrayed and broken-hearted friend. It is all a part of you. Everything did happen for a reason known to your soul. The tiles of memory and experience dance before you, coming together in a striking masterpiece.

While in this state of connectedness, ask any questions you may have of Spirit or your highest self. Allow the answers to flow to you, as a breeze would glide across the water. Spend time with your mosaic, expressing gratitude for every experience you have witnessed. These pieces of your past are vital to honor, yet not to cling to forever.

Now visualize all you will do in the future. Climb mountains? Travel to distant lands? Run a marathon? Picture yourself in jubilant celebration of living an active, joyful life. Imagine the people and events of the times yet to come. Who will you meet next? Who will you love? What will you change about your behavior or beliefs? There is no limit to the possibilities of your life. You are the author of the novel and the composer of the song. It is time to see all you are capable of in a Universe of infinite potential.

Take a long, deep breath and begin to come back to the present moment. You feel beautiful and revitalized. Thank Spirit and yourself for this intricate mosaic meditation. Slowly open your eyes and take another breath, stretching your muscles and soaking in the radiance of the energy you've ignited. Your intuitive heart is glowing brightly as you resume the rest of your day. Take time to write your experiences and reflections in your HeartGlow journal. Be sure to make note of any messages or symbols you need to be mindful of. Meditation is a gift we can give ourselves every day. Whether you have five minutes or an hour to sit in contemplation, take the opportunity to connect in this sacred space.

EXERCISE 16: GRATITUDE INVENTORY

Reflecting on what we are thankful for in our lives is a powerful way to shift our perspective from the isolated self to a broader view of universal connectedness. Expressing gratitude for the great number of blessings in our world reminds us of the gifts we are being given by Spirit on a daily basis. Whether it is the air we breathe, clothes on our back, or a person to love, we all have things to be grateful for.

Recent research at the University of California, Davis, indicates people who are grateful have a higher sense of well-being, security, health, and happiness.[1] Theorists are only beginning to investigate the positive benefits of this essential emotion, but they have been intuitively known in spiritual circles for centuries. By freely expressing our gratitude, we welcome the miraculous energy of love and abundance into our lives, giving us even more blessings to count. We create our own reality through the devoted expression of thankfulness.

In your HeartGlow journal, I would like you to record your blessings. Take an inventory of what you are grateful for in your life. This is not meant to be a casual list of a few names and events. Please examine your life in detail and write down all things that come to mind for which you are thankful. Remember our burdens are often a piece of good fortune, as they provide opportunities for learning and growth. Your list should be comprehensive and may include hundreds of items or more. It may be easier for you to divide your list into categories, such as home, family, friends, work, nature, and so on.

I am not going to restrict you in any way, as your creative process is uniquely yours and a true expression of your soul. Some folks list items simply—such as "my child"—while others prefer to describe their blessing in greater detail by writing "the sweet smile of my daughter when she is sleeping." Either way is fine, although do not hesitate to let your artistry flow. A number of HeartGlow clients have taken this exercise to the next level by writing songs, poetry, and even creating an art piece from the inspiration of their gratitude inventory.

If you have difficulty doing this exercise at all, then try again another day. We all have days when we feel burdened by life and not especially blessed. Do not let a difficult day deter you from experiencing this exercise. I find completing a gratitude inventory is best done over a period of time, so give yourself a week to work on it. Simply assign dedicated pages in your journal and add to the list whenever you choose. I would like you to revisit your list once a week, taking in the energy of your blessings. Please reflect on your life's recent events, and then add a new item of gratitude to the inventory each week thereafter.

The gratitude inventory is a pleasant and simple exercise to share with your children in a creative way. If you choose to do so, I suggest encouraging your child to draw what they're thankful for using colored paper and crayons and then posting the results in their room. We can raise our children to recognize and develop a deep sense of gratitude. Its expression need not be relegated to one Thursday in November, where it shares the stage with roast turkey and football. Each day we are blessed with the opportunity to live a vibrant life; it is our choice whether we decide to do so. Keep a gratitude inventory throughout your life and look back over it as a powerful reflection of your own spiritual development.

SUMMARY OF KEY POINTS

Discovering the bliss of intuitive parenting comes more easily to those who have balance in their lives. Maintaining a dedicated perspective on well-being enables you as a parent to fully nurture your children: mind, body, and spirit. To expect peace and wellness for your family, you must demonstrate and exude your own intentions. Actions do speak louder than words and should be in alignment with your intentions. Energy speaks even louder, making any contradiction extremely obvious. Living a conscious life, mindful and focused, allows your Divine light to brilliantly shine and be the best example for your child.

Self-healing begins with the firm belief that you are the creator of your own life and have the ability to manifest lasting change in your world. Knowing that the blessing and responsibility lies only with you is liberating, and also intimidating. Moving forward with a healthy, balanced perspective first requires you to release your attachments to the past and the future. Allow yourself to let go of the baggage of unrealized expectations, toxic relationships, labels, and societal projections. If this is difficult to even consider, you need to recognize *you are more than the story you tell.*

The daily responsibilities and burdens, which confront all families, can be considerable and are often magnified when a family member is also living with a chronic illness or disability. Although we have all felt alone, misunderstood, and overwhelmed by life's journey at times, we must remember we are one with the All, brilliantly interconnected by the intuitive energy of our hearts. Being mindful and proactive on all levels of causation is the clear path to wellness. Knowing our state of health physically, mentally, emotionally, and spiritually allows us to take the responsibility in our own hands and create a life of peace, balance, and clarity. Experiencing less pain, increased vitality, and reduced stress enables us to be the best intuitive parents we can be.

HEARTGLOW HINTS FOR INTUITIVE PARENTING

- Establish your family's healthy routines for eating, sleeping, and exercise. It all begins with self-care and being a beacon of light for the ones we love.
- Schedule time each week to be alone. Take a walk, ponder nature—simply be.
- Know when to call in the support network. There are times we all need encouragement and reinforcement in our lives.
- Empower yourself by releasing the need to be everything to everyone.
- Exude the love, peace, and clarity you intend for your family.

9

Living with an Intuitive Heart

How far you go in life depends on your being tender with the young,
compassionate with the aged, sympathetic with the striving and
tolerant of the weak and strong. Because someday in life you will
have been all of these.

GEORGE WASHINGTON CARVER,
AMERICAN SCIENTIST (1864–1943)

A new way of life awaits you when you live with an intuitive heart—an existence filled with love, guidance, and forgiveness, a life aligned and immersed in the Divine flow. Throughout this book we have explored the research, theories, techniques, and personal stories behind employing our subtle energy systems to benefit our families. We should be confident in the fact that we are graced with energy fields, energy centers, and energy pathways, which help process, decode, and explore the intricate nuances of universal vibration.

We've discovered the Field of Intuitive Harmony, the special place our hearts meet. When in resonance within this field, we appreciate the more subtle energies of those we care about, opening the door to enhanced communication and healing. We've learned to foster even greater resonance through techniques of sound, touch, and love. The concepts of sensory exploration, curbing the ego, and achieving emotional stability allow us to establish a common language of energy with our loved ones. HeartGlow intuitive parenting ushers in a new wave of health, connectedness, and prosperity for our families. You need only put what you have learned into practice to be successful.

EMBRACING OUR WORLD

Life at home has taken on a new air of peace and calm. Raegan's health is stable, and for the past several years she has needed little medical intervention other than the occasional pediatric checkup. Don't get me wrong—her physical and developmental disabilities are profound and quite challenging. As we had been told at the time of her birth, her small, malformed brain has left her extremely compromised. Although the doctors continue to predict a short life expectancy, we try not to dwell on the unknown, opting instead to leave any prognosis up to Raegan. We have learned to embrace our world, taking each day as it comes, thankful and blessed to be together, not allowing fear of the future to interfere with our joy of the present moment. We choose to leave our feelings of victimization behind to step into our life with acceptance, grace, and love.

With our heart communication in constant flow, I now rely on it as much as I do my other senses. It has become an intricate part of our relationship and is employed effortlessly. In fact, Raegan has taught quite a few people in her life how to live this way. Mark, who never considered himself to be intuitive, has opened his heart and mind to the possibilities and now greatly enjoys the benefits. A few of our nurses also enjoy a deep connection with Raegan and report instances of specific energy communication. I know our Field of Intuitive Harmony grows stronger with love, experience, and intention. There are times I recognize I am conversing directly with my little girl, as the topic is age appropriate and timely. Other moments, however, her messages take on the tone of a wise elder, and I am aware she is sharing her soul's wisdom with me.

One evening Raegan and I were snuggling in my room just prior to going to bed. Sitting her up on my lap, I began talking to our reflection in the mirrored closet door just a few feet away. "What a beautiful girl you are! Can you see that gorgeous Angel-Baby in the mirror?" I asked playfully. Bouncing her around a bit to help her eye catch the motion, I realized she could not see what I could. Raegan was not able to catch sight of us in the mirror. Although she smiled at the energy and tone of my voice, I became painfully aware she could not see her own reflection. We had been told her vision was impaired to some degree, but the idea of Raegan not seeing herself struck me as incredibly sad.

"Oh, Raegan," I cried. "I can't believe you will never get to see your own beauty!" Tears flowed heavily from my eyes as I sniffled and gently cradled my daughter. Feeling extremely sorry for us both, I continued to whimper and cry as I placed her down on the bed. Like a lightning bolt through me, Raegan's voice echoed inside my heart, "Which one of us truly sees their own beauty?" I paused for a moment to contemplate her profound statement, thinking of the numerous times I had seen myself and other people put ourselves down while looking in the mirror, never appreciating our own inner or outer beauty. Raegan was right. Our vision, skewed by ego and acutely focused on the physical realm, can blind us to the immense beauty that resides within us all. Raegan's frail body may not have sight, but her higher self has perception.

The most rewarding aspect of my professional intuitive parenting work is sharing the knowledge and possibilities with other families. It has been my greatest pleasure to ignite the intuitive hearts of others and see them achieve significant results. Raegan and I are not an isolated case. We are just like you, but due to the circumstance of her disability, we needed to find an alternate and creative way to communicate. Parents everywhere are using their subtle energy systems to bring about dramatic improvement in their family life. Whether the people involved are teenagers with behavior issues, overstimulated toddlers, special-needs families, or newborn babies, intuitive parenting techniques can implement positive transformations in the way you live.

Gail, a single mother of three children, contacted me to help address a variety of issues in her household. She was overwhelmed by the responsibility of caring for three very different children and felt growing resentment about the situation. Somewhere along the line, she had lost her sense of self and allowed the children's energies to take over the house and her entire life. Always in a state of chaos and reaction, she was not able to get clarity and balance for her family and didn't feel confident in her decisions.

Gail made the commitment to examine her life from a higher place and began living each day listening to her intuitive heart. As she progressed further in her HeartGlow journey, she was able to see her life from an energetic and spiritual perspective, making needed changes in the way she interacted with her children and organized their environment. Her revitalized sense of self and emotional healing have allowed Gail to tap into her own higher sense of knowing and be a confident, happy mom once again.

Tom was frustrated and concerned with his twelve-year-old son's ever-growing behavioral issues. The child was often abusive to his siblings and constantly got into trouble at school. It seemed the family had tried everything to find peace and balance, to no avail. Through his intuitive parenting exploration, Tom was able to identify quite a few energetic triggers for his son. He chose to implement positive changes in their home and family diet. As he gained greater insight to his son's emotional challenges through meditation and visualization, a dialogue opened between the two of them. The volatility and frustration disappeared. Tom now reports that he and his son have never been closer.

An emotional and profound demonstration of the power of motherly love was shown to me prior to launching my career as an intuitive consultant. Shortly after Raegan's birth, while I was still working at the insurance company, I had a vivid dream about my co-worker, Jane. In my dream, she was dressed in a gorgeous wedding gown and was posing in front of a mirror. I was looking down from above at her and felt such love, pride, and adoration. The next day at the office, I was informed it was Jane's birthday. "Happy birthday!" I said to Jane. "Wow! I had a dream about you last night. Isn't that strange I would dream about you on your birthday?"

I began to tell her all the details of the dream and the fact I felt a connection as if she was my daughter, which was odd as Jane was a number of years older than I was. "Oh no . . . wait a minute. I wasn't myself in the dream. I was *your* mother!" I said triumphantly, as realization dawned on me. "I was your mother looking down at you and appreciating how beautiful you looked in your wedding gown! Yeah, that's it," I continued.

"Deb, do you know what you're saying?" Jane asked. Tears slid down her cheeks as she carefully explained the details of her family situation. Her much beloved mother had died when Jane was a young woman and never got to see her marry or have children. She continued to say she'd had lunch with her sister the weekend before and talked at length about their mother and all the times they missed sharing. Feeling a deep sense of melancholy, she went home and prayed to her mother, expressing her intense longing to feel connected with her, asking if she knew about her marriage and life with her family. Jane needed to know if her mother was watching over her.

The answer came through the channel of me, just a few days later. Her mother responded to her daughter's direct question by sending a beautiful vision of Jane's wedding day with every detail intact. She was indeed watching over her daughter with great affection. It was a significant and moving experience for both Jane and me, as we realized the eternal power of love knows no boundaries. Whether in Heaven or on Earth, our soul connections are everlasting.

THE HEARTGLOW WAY

Choosing happiness as a way of life ultimately leads to the understanding that joy is our natural state of being.
—MICHAEL BERNARD BECKWITH, *SPIRITUAL LIBERATION*

My personal journey into a life of intuitive parenting has been filled with poignant encounters, moments of intense emotion, and glimmering flashes of mystical expression. My family has learned through direct experience the wonder, possibility, and miracles available to us through listening and speaking with our intuitive hearts. We are all naturally designed by Divine grace to attune to the higher vibrations of the energetic realms and can utilize this connection for healing and enhanced communication. However, to allow this magic into your life, you must clear away the static from your personal channel and be open to receive.

The global significance of parent-child energy communication became especially vivid to me when I started receiving notes from people all over the world who share similar experiences with their children. Regardless of culture, religion, or social status, parents were able to appreciate the subtle energies of their families. Their anecdotal stories were like my own and gave practical credence to the numerous theories of resonance and entanglement. A common frustration, however, seemed to be the inconsistency of reception. How could they make positive changes in their lives to encourage the frequency and accuracy of heart communication?

Through experience with my clients and in my own life, I believe there is a strong correlation between heightened consciousness and successful intuitive parenting. The more aware and cognizant you are of life and the world around you, the greater your results. You increase your energy sensitivity by clearing away the chaos of harsh judgment and limited belief. By being mindful of your thoughts, decisions, and actions, you shine your inner light and raise your vibration. Here you will find nine key components I find essential to living the glorious, happy life of intuitive parenting, the HeartGlow way.

THE HEARTGLOW WAY TO INTUITIVE PARENTING

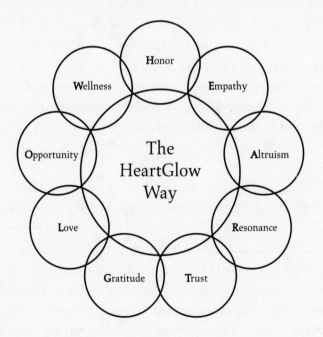

Honor

Living a life of honor is to demonstrate truth, honesty, and integrity in your actions and beliefs. We often relate to the concept of honor when making a pledge to our country or taking a matrimonial vow, but do we consider honoring our soul's path each and every day? Allow your choices and behavior to reflect the best parts of you and also take responsibility when your actions affect another. When living with great respect for every soul, you begin to see the world as an amazing opportunity to share love. Recognizing and honoring the light within others allows a closeness and reverence beyond typical experience and vastly benefits our families.

By honoring Raegan as a vibrant soul on her own journey, I have been able to appreciate the significance of her life and its effect on others, moving past the limited place of asking "why did this happen to us?" to an expansive view of love's higher calling. I believe it has shifted the focus from a *me* perspective to one of seeing the vast interconnected hearts of us all. Honoring the light within by being authentic leads to a magnificent life.

Empathy

Empathy is the ability to feel, sense, or relate to the experiences of others—knowing what it is like to walk in their shoes or wear their hats, so to speak. Having understanding and compassion for the actions and behaviors of those we encounter infuses us with a deep sense of connectedness. We demonstrate a higher awareness when we leave harsh judgments behind and opt instead to empathize with others. Our children are better served when we can lovingly connect with their energy signature and try to see from their unique perspective. Allow your intuitive heart to lead the way to a life of sweet understanding.

My ability to empathize with others has brought me peace. There have been a significant number of encounters throughout my life when people have been harmful, disloyal, or even downright cruel. By sliding into their loafers for a moment or two, I was able to see the circumstances that brought them to their actions. Theirs were maybe not the choices I would have made, but I understand they were doing what they could in the moment, and I try to avoid passing judgment. Empathy has given me the freedom to forgive others and myself.

ALTRUISM

The concept of altruism is living a life in benefit of the interests of others—being of service to society and the world without gain to the self. This is a foundation belief in numerous religions, such as Christianity, Buddhism, and Judaism. Think of altruism as simply being nice and kind to those around you without regard to a payoff for yourself. It is not being a servant to someone or under the influence of another's control. We raise our personal vibration when we open our hearts in love and service to others. Demonstrating this behavior to our children is the best way to nurture their internal sense of benevolence and generosity.

We all have daily opportunities to be caring to one another. It is simple to make the choice to offer kindness in place of indifference. Step away from the pull of ego and act with your heart. Today, more than any other, we need to foster service and compassion in our world. It is up to us to create a society built on the foundations of unity, peace, and caring. Begin where you are and allow it to spread like the ripples caused by a tiny pebble cast in water.

RESONANCE

We have learned resonance is our energetic connection to someone or something, when we are in harmony with another, tuned into and affected by the same frequency, vibration, or wavelength. Having a practical understanding of this key component is vital to intuitive parenting, as it acknowledges our ability to have an effect within our Field of Intuitive Harmony and in our homes. Respecting and nurturing our energetic connections are the next transcendental steps in parenting. Being mindful of your own energy signature and sensitive to your child's empowers a family to live a vibrant life in brilliant intuitive harmony. Imagine what your family will be able to do when you foster resonance in your home. There is no limit to what can be, as love knows no bounds.

TRUST

When we speak of trust, we are referring to reliance on a belief—having faith and conviction in someone or something. When living an intuitive life, you need to rely not only on yourself but also in the phenomenal possibilities inherent in the Universe. We are stepping away from boundaries and allowing God's grace to take a higher role in our lives. Trusting the subtle cues within your own physical and energetic fields fosters confidence and accuracy of skill as well as certainty in knowing that whatever is occurring in your world from moment to moment is by Divine design. Trust your children and they will trust you.

Trust *yourself* and do not allow your ego urgings or those of another to dictate your course. Find the balance of incorporating intuitive insights with learned knowledge. You are not abandoning your intellect and experience, you are merely adding a new tool to put into practice and trust.

GRATITUDE

Gratitude is the emotion and energy we exude when in deep appreciation of the circumstances in our world. Long embraced as an essential virtue in philosophy and countless religions, thankfulness leads to a life of peace, health, and prosperity. Being grateful for the diverse experiences of living directly correlates to success in achievement, well-being, and social bonding. Regardless of your family's challenges or blessings, instilling a sense of gratitude for the miracle of life itself raises your energetic vibration, fostering resonance in the Field of Intuitive Harmony. Be grateful for what is and experience the wonder of Heaven on Earth.

I am immensely grateful for the assorted events and experiences in my life. What at one time I deemed to be burdens or hardships, I now consider blessings of pure transformation. My sense of gratitude seems to grow each day as new people, situations, and encounters come forth, bringing magic and mystery. It is all such a fantastic adventure! Start life anew by celebrating the amazement that surrounds you.

LOVE

The Divine Spirit is the manifestation and source of all love in the Universe, magnificently expressing itself in the smile of a child, a butterfly on the breeze, and the majesty of a mountain range. We each are creative expressions of love. Demonstrating, supporting, and celebrating love is the meaning and purpose of all life. It is a choice to allow our loving God light to shine through our actions, intentions, and relationships. Do we choose to exude grace and to live a life of love? Allow the beautiful creative force of love to transform your world from a fearful struggle to a heart-glowing, peaceful existence.

My life completely blossomed when I began to comprehend the power of unconditional love. My daughter has taught me what love is and what it is not. Opening my heart to this higher vibration has allowed even more affection to come to me, including sensing for the first time in my thirties the immeasurable pleasure, liberation, and fulfillment of self-love. I finally understood the adage, "You can not truly love another until you first love yourself."

OPPORTUNITY

Opportunity is our chance to make use of the circumstances in our life. We often associate this concept only with positive experiences, such as an offer of employment or being selected to receive a scholarship. It is, however, so much more. I see our everyday conditions and occurrences, even situations we deem negative, to be opportunities for growth and enlightenment. We choose whether or not to take advantage of what comes before us, taking to heart the old saying that we should make lemonade from sour lemons. The freedom and opportunity to expand our perceptions and live a new life of intuitive parenting are ours, if we choose to seize the day.

This book and my work as an intuitive consultant are clear examples of how I have found opportunity in a challenging situation. Choosing to see my life in a new way and share my daughter's teachings with you is making lemonade. I might have taken a different course by crippling myself with grief, anger, and the weight of victimization. Fortunately, Raegan's persistence and guiding light encouraged my soul to persevere and answer the higher calling. Never underestimate how the choices you make can affect another. We are all partners in an elegant cosmic dance.

WELLNESS

Making a commitment to wellness is crucial when integrating intuitive parenting techniques. We must have a healthy respect of our bodies, minds, and spirits, knowing our entire being is an instrument of subtle energy. Even if we live with chronic illness or disability, we are perfect and exactly as God intended. You can embrace well-being by demonstrating proper care. Be mindful of what you eat, how you move, and the amount of rest you get. Take time to process your emotions and release any negativity trapped in your body. The beautiful temple of you will appreciate your devoted gesture. Loving care for your child is enhanced when you also nurture yourself.

Although, admittedly, I could be more diligent in my eating and exercise habits, my overall health and well-being have greatly improved as I strive for balance in all aspects of my life. As I have honed my psychic skills over the years, I do find they improve when I am at my best physically, mentally, and emotionally. When the vehicle of my soul is in proper working order, my vibration is higher, allowing greater sensitivity to energy cues. Your energetic body is a part of you, so clear away the toxins and excess debris to enhance your intuitive opportunities.

Intuitive parenting is a sacred journey in establishing higher levels of spiritual connection/communion with our children through celebration and exploration of the Divine energy within—when our inner light recognizes the internal glow of our child and utilizes the connection for communication and healing. The nine elements of HeartGlow are meant to be the philosophical starting point for you to see all life with greater significance.

We must realize the way we live our lives greatly affects everything around us, including our children. Our choices, behaviors, thoughts, emotions, actions, and habits all interweave to create our existence, our individual mosaic or tapestry. The subtle energy system is only as healthy as the time, love, and intention we put into it. You will reap the fantastic rewards of an intuitive connection with your child if you apply these concepts with dedication into your daily living. The choice to become an intuitive parent is yours.

HeartGlow Exercises

It is no small commitment to live a life of love, truth, integrity, and honor; to resonate at a higher level of vibration, living consciously with full awareness of and responsibility for your actions and behaviors. It is a path that, once started, you do not depart from, as you begin to appreciate all the true beauty the Universe has intended for you and your family. You discover the amazement, wonder, and grace of personal freedom and unique expression as you let go of labels, harsh judgments, and negative stories to step into the bliss of your energetic life. These final two exercises help you put into practice the intuitive parenting skills you have learned.

Exercise 17: A HeartGlow Energy Audit

In this exercise I would like you to take an energy audit of your life. Literally examine your daily environment, habits, relationships, and behavior to determine how energy plays a role in your family. You will quickly find—since we are all energetic beings living in an energetic world—energy is everything and everywhere. Now are *you* ready to improve the quality of your life by incorporating the exercises and lessons you have learned in this book? Are you ready to free yourself of ego's hold, radiate your vibrant hue, and be an intuitive parent?

For this exercise, you will need your HeartGlow journal and privacy to do some soul searching. As with our other exercises, begin with the HeartGlow Primer to put yourself in a balanced, relaxed, and receptive state. I would like you to complete an energy audit chart for your family. Take a look at each person individually to determine areas in life to improve and then assign an energy

Family Member	Challenge/Opportunity	Activity/Solution
Mom	Stress	Meditation & walking
Dad	Anger	Visualization & breathing
Suzy	Hyperactive	Aura wash
Tommy	Nonverbal	Point-to-point

lesson to implement positive change. List the challenges, opportunities, and areas of concern and then the activities, behaviors, and concrete actions you can make to start your family on the Heart-Glow path. The chart below is an example. When you are ready to begin, open your journal and design an audit chart specialized to your family.

The chart above is merely a sample to give you an idea of how to complete the audit. Please design your own chart with your family's issues and concerns in mind. This exercise is meant to give you a starting point on what you can do to assist your family and yourself on this journey. Flip through the book to identify specific exercises that would address issues your family is facing. If you know where your challenges are, then it is easier to find solutions.

Our best intentions are only manifest if our dedicated actions support them.

You will find yourself adjusting this chart as you and your family evolve in the HeartGlow process. Seeing the techniques work in your life gives you the motivation to apply them in other areas of concern. Always know your intuitive heart will not steer you wrong. Take the time to listen to the slow stirrings of your soul, which are ever present in the vibrancy of you.

Intention	Actions
Go back to school.	Pick up a catalog, apply for aid, and enroll in a class.
Change jobs.	Update resume, secure references, and apply.
Lose weight.	Visit the doctor, join a support group, and walk daily.

EXERCISE 18: INTENTIONS FOR HEARTGLOW LIVING

In this final exercise, I would like you to set your intentions for your family and yourself. Please record in your HeartGlow journal exactly what you wish for your life in regards to health, happiness, abundance, education, and all other aspects. Be precise. Set a specific intention in writing for each area you wish to explore, and then beside that on the page write three actions you can take now in support of the intention. For example,

Write as many intentions as you would like, being sure to always write three actions in support of the intention. We must get in the habit of empowering ourselves to move forward. A dream remains only a dream if there are no steps toward manifestation and positive energy behind it. By being open to experiences and taking risks, you are giving yourself the gift of enhanced opportunity. Using the same example as above, you would not earn a scholarship or meet that benefactor in the financial aid office if you never went in to apply. Believe in yourself and give the Universe the opportunity to work with you, to make your dreams come true.

You can teach your children this same technique of using intentions in their world. They may enjoy creating art projects or songs of their heart's desire. The sky is the limit as to how you do this, so follow your intuitive parenting sense. I strongly suggest you avoid making wish lists of material things, for it is what the thing represents that is the heart of the matter. If it is abundance or security you desire, then state it as such, followed by the three actions you can take to manifest it.

If you desire luxuries to make yourself feel or look better, then there are ego issues to explore, and self-worth would be a good intention to focus on. As you move forward on your intuitive parenting journey, you will discover that material things become less important to you. Although you will have a heightened sense of appreciation for all things, monetary value seems to pertain less and less. Enjoy the exploration and have fun living, loving, and growing with an intuitive heart.

SUMMARY OF KEY POINTS

A new way of life awaits you when you live with an intuitive heart: an existence filled with love, guidance, grace, and forgiveness; a life aligned and immersed in the Divine flow. HeartGlow intuitive parenting ushers in a new wave of health, connectedness, and prosperity for families. You need only put what you have learned into practice to be successful. We are all naturally designed by Divine grace to attune to the higher vibrations of the energetic realms and can utilize this connection for healing and enhanced communication. However, to allow this magic into your life, you must clear away the static from your personal channel and be open to receive.

Regardless of culture, religion, or social status, parents are able to appreciate the subtle energies of their families. Anecdotal stories give practical credence to the numerous theories of resonance and entanglement. There is a strong correlation between heightened consciousness and successful intuitive parenting. The more aware and cognizant you are of life and the world around you, the greater your results. You can increase energy sensitivity by clearing away the chaos of harsh judgment and limited belief. Shine your brilliant light by being mindful of your thoughts, decisions, and actions. The nine key components of honor, empathy, altruism, resonance, trust, gratitude, love, opportunity, and wellness are essential to living the glorious, happy life of intuitive parenting, the HeartGlow way.

HEARTGLOW HINTS FOR INTUITIVE PARENTING

- Trust yourself and the internal guidance you are receiving.
- Listen more than you speak. It is amazing what can be heard when you immerse yourself in silence.
- Allow your courageous heart to live in the authenticity of truth and love.
- We all radiate a unique reflection of light. Appreciate the diversity of the hues around you and release the desire to control others.
- Each day we make choices how we live our lives. Choose from your highest place, honoring the integrity of the Divine Spirit within us all.

We have come to the place in our time together where you must step forward to implement these new skills into your life. Have faith in yourself, knowing you are a radiant light of God, living out the Divine plan you have created. You have the intuitive tools and energy strengths to handle anything that comes your way. Everything in your world is there for a reason. The people, places, and even hardships are your opportunities for growth and soul evolution. You now know you are more than any role you play, story you tell, or label once assigned. If you are unhappy with your life, you have the power and freedom to make another choice. You create your bliss.

My daughter, Raegan, has taught me much on this intricate journey of ours. She has shown me how to love, believe in God, and detach from my anger, fear, and frustration. Her smile and effervescent spirit are ideal demonstrations of perfection in imperfection—she does not allow her fragile, broken body to dim the brilliant light of her soul. These intuitive parenting lessons come to you because she was able to teach me how to listen and speak with my heart. Your child, just like mine, has a vibrant soul connection to you and has much to teach. Energy is available to us all. We need only ignite the glow of our intuitive hearts to experience the power and beauty of our energetic connections.

Notes

Chapter 2

1. Jon Klimo, *Channeling* (Berkeley: North Atlantic Books, 1998), 366.

2. Rollin McCraty, Mike Atkinson, and Raymond Trevor Bradley, "Electrophysiological Evidence of Intuition: Part 2. A System Wide Process?," *The Journal of Alternative and Complementary Medicine* 10, no. 2 (2004): 325–336.

Chapter 3

1. Rupert Sheldrake, "Apparent Telepathy Between Babies and Nursing Mothers: A Survey." *Journal of the Society for Psychical Research* 66 (2002): 181–185.

2. _____ "Morphic Fields and Morphic Resonance: An Introduction." *Rupert Sheldrake, biologist & author* (2005), http://www.sheldrake.org/Articles&Papers/papers/morphic/morphic_intro.html (accessed March 2009).

3. Gregg Braden, *The Divine Matrix* (Carlsbad, Calif.: Hay House, 2006), 143.

Chapter 4

1. Elizabeth and Derek Rintel, "Sound Therapy for the Learning Disabled Child," *Sound Therapy International* (1995), http://www.soundtherapyinternational.com/images/rintel_study_1995.pdf.

2. Jonathan Goldman, "Overview Sound Healing," *Jonathan Goldman's Healing Sounds* (2006), http://www.healingsounds.com/articles/overview-sound-healing.asp.

3. M. Tylee, M. R. Popovic, S. Yu, and C. Craven, "Human Responses to Vibration Therapy," *Engineering in Medicine and Biology Society* 2 (2003): 1705–1708.

4. Walter Weston, *Pray Well* (Wadsworth, Ohio: Transitions Press, 1996), 56–59.

Chapter 5

1. Touch Research Institute, http://www.miami.edu/touch-research.

2. Michael H. Cohen, Kathi J. Kemper, Laura Stevens, Dean Hashimoto, and Joan Gilmour, "Pediatric Use of Complementary Therapies: Ethical and Policy Choices," *Pediatrics* 116, no 4 (2005): 568–575.

3. Barbara Ann Brennan, *Hands of Light* (New York: Bantam, 1987), 147.

4. Diane Stein, *Essential Reiki* (Berkeley: Crossing Press, 1995), 12.

5. Philip Chan, MD, "Reiki and the Conventional Health Care Provider Recommendations and Potholes," *The International Center for Reiki Training* (1990–2005), http://www.reiki.org/reikinews/reikin10.html (accessed March 2009).

6. Hans Van Leeuwen, "Investigations into Reiki and Its Use in Hospitals," *The Healing Pages* (2002-2005), http://www.thehealingpages.com/Articles/ReikiinHospitals.html.

Chapter 6

1. The Institute for Research on Unlimited Love. "Mission," http://www.unlimitedloveinstitute.org/mission/index.html.

2. AngelBabyMoms. http://angelbabymoms.com.

3. Deepak Chopra, *The Book of Secrets* (New York: Harmony, 2004), 152.

4. August T. Jaccaci, *General Periodicity* (Scarborough, Maine: Fiddlehead, 2000), 69.

5. J. Kristeller and T. J. Johnson, "Cultivating Loving-Kindness: A Two-Stage Model for the Effects of Meditation on Compassion, Altruism and Spirituality," paper presented, Scientific and Religious Perspectives on Altruism, Philadelphia, Pa., June 2003.

Chapter 8

1. Robert A. Emmons and Michael E. McCullough, "Highlights from the Research Project on Gratitude and Thankfulness," *The Department of Psychology, University of California, Davis*, http://psychology.ucdavis.edu/labs/emmons (accessed November 2009).

Glossary

Affirmation: A simple, positive statement that asserts something is true. By employing affirmations, we reprogram the mind with statements of positive thoughts, which create and attract everything we desire to manifest in our lives.

Attunement: An initiation that creates a healer by the passing down of energy from master to student.

Aura: Also known as an energy field or biofield, it encompasses all living things and can provide clues to the health and overall well-being of a person or thing. It is a multidimensional, radiant pool of energy that envelops you and can extend dozens of feet beyond your body in a large oval or egg shape.

Chakra: Any of the seven central points of energy activity in our bodies and subtle energy systems. Chakras are responsible for decoding, exploring, and processing the life force energy we encounter. Also referred to as *energy centers*.

Channeling: Being able to act as a vehicle for thoughts, pictures, emotions, and information that are coming from a source outside the self and not from traditional means of perception. Intuition, ESP, telepathy, and heart communication are all forms of channeling. Also known as *energy communication*.

Clairaudience (clear hearing): The ability to hear information from outside sources, almost like a special inner ear.

Clairsentience (clear feeling): When intuitive information resides in a person's energy field and is then delivered to the conscious mind by a cue from the physical body.

Clairvoyance (clear seeing): Intuitive information coming to us clearly and concisely through dreams, mental images, and creative insights. We see this information with the mind's eye, like a movie or a symbolic picture.

Creative Visualization: A technique that utilizes the power of the imagination to manifest balance and healing in life.

Energy: Our great power within; the Divine Life Force. It is our capacity to connect with and be part of the Higher Consciousness on all levels of existence. It is known throughout the world by many names, such as *Prana*, *Qi*, *Chi*, *Ki*, and the *Universal Life Force*.

Energy centers: Commonly referred to as chakras, they are the central points of energy activity in our bodies and subtle energy systems and are responsible for decoding, exploring, and processing the life force energy we encounter.

Energy field: The human energy field, also known as the aura or biofield, encompasses all living things and can provide clues to the health and overall well-being of a person or thing. It is a multi-dimensional, radiant pool of energy that envelops you and can extend dozens of feet beyond your body in a large oval or egg shape.

Energy pathway: Channels by which energies flow within our subtle energy system. These channels form a web that connects and communicates with the hundreds of energy centers within us, distributing subtle energy signals to all major systems and organs of our physical bodies. Also referred to as *nadis* or *meridians*.

Field of Intuitive Harmony: The common energy field created by the sacred bond between loved ones. This is the place where our hearts meet.

HeartGlow: The conscious awareness of Divine energy radiating from our core, when our essence (or God light) emits its unique glow out to the receptive, loving Universe and receives guidance, love, and support in return. When you live your life with a glowing heart, you are making a choice to access and flow with Divine energy.

HeartGlow Primer: This is a starting point for most of our HeartGlow exercises to get into a receptive, relaxed state. It is also beneficial to do on its own whenever you need to stop the chaos and reconnect with Source.

Glossary

Intuition: A form of perception often referred to as the sixth sense or soul sense. Intuitive perception is a complete body process involving a number of human systems that operate in conjunction to receive, process, and decode information.

Intuitive parenting: A style of parenting in which you apply a form of deep insight, a heightened perception of the world around you, for the enrichment of your family and yourself.

Meditation: An exercise that enables us to connect with the Divine Energy through deep relaxation and the absence of active thought. It is the process of quieting the mind to expand awareness and break loose from the bonds of mental and emotional attachments.

Meridians: Channels by which energies flow within our subtle energy system. These channels form a web that connects and communicates with the hundreds of energy centers within us, distributing subtle energy signals to all major systems and organs of our physical bodies. Also referred to as *energy pathways* or *nadis*.

Music therapy: A well-established healthcare profession that utilizes music to address emotional, social, physical, and cognitive needs of patients in all age groups.

Nadis: Another word for energy pathways or meridians. It is from the root *nad* in Sanskrit, which translates to "channel" or "flow."

Reiki: An ancient healing art that was brought to the forefront in the 1800s by Mikao Usui, who received knowledge of this energy healing technique after a twenty-one-day meditation on Mount Koriyama in Japan.

Glossary

Resonance: Being tuned into and affected by the energetic frequency, vibration, or wavelength shared by someone else. Often commonly expressed as being "on the same wavelength" or sharing a "vibe."

Self-healing: The ability to manifest wellness and lasting change in your world by being mindful and proactive in all aspects of life. Knowing our state of health physically, mentally, emotionally, and spiritually allows us to take the responsibility in our own hands and create a life of peace, balance, and clarity.

Sensory exploration approach: A commitment to using our senses in a heightened state of awareness, to perceive with every part of our being as an instrument of Spirit. This sensory method develops an energy language within your own family. Through sharing common experiences with sharp awareness, we create an energy repertoire unique to our own Field of Intuitive Harmony.

Sound therapy: A healing modality in which sound or vibration addresses deficient health conditions in people.

Spiritual attachment: Loving our children at the highest levels possible, in which we experience the levels beyond personality and ego.

Touch therapy: A healing modality in which touch is used to addresses deficient health conditions in people.

Vibration therapy: A healing modality that utilizes vibration to address deficient health conditions in people.

Suggested Reading

Bartlett, Richard. *Matrix Energetics*. New York: Atria Books/Beyond Words, 2007.

Beck, Martha. *Expecting Adam*. New York: Berkley, 1999.

Brennan, Barbara Ann. *Hands of Light*. New York: Bantam, 1988.

Chopra, Deepak. *The Book of Secrets*. New York: Harmony, 2004.

Dyer, Wayne. *The Power of Intention*. Carlsbad, Calif.: Hay House, 2004.

Gawain, Shakti. *Living in the Light*. Novato, Calif.: New World Library, 1998.

Suggested Reading

Hawkes, Joyce Whiteley. *Cell-Level Healing*. New York: Atria Books/Beyond Words, 2006.

Jenkins, Peggy Joy. *Nurturing Spirituality in Children*. New York: Atria Books/Beyond Words, 2008.

Judith, Anodea. *Wheels of Life*. St. Paul, Minn.: Llewellyn, 1987.

McTaggart, Lynne. *The Field*. New York: Harper, 2002.

Paulson, Genevieve. *Kundalini and the Chakras*. St. Paul, Minn.: Llewellyn, 2002.

Sherwood, Keith. *Chakra Therapy*. St. Paul, Minn.: Llewellyn, 2002.